MEETING JOHN WIMBER

Meeting John Wimber

Edited by
JOHN GUNSTONE

SCB Publishers

MONARCH
Crowborough

First published 1996

British Library Cataloguing Data
A catalogue record for this book is available
from the British Library

ISBN 1 85424 350 0

Co-published in South Africa with
SCB Publishers
Cornelis Struik House, 80 McKenzie Street
Cape Town 8001, South Africa.
Reg no 04/02203/06

Designed and produced by Bookprint Creative Services
P.O. Box 827, BN21 3YJ, England for
MONARCH PUBLICATIONS
Broadway House, The Broadway,
Crowborough, E. Sussex, TN6 1HQ
Printed in Great Britain.

Contents

CHAPTER ONE

John Gunstone

John Gunstone (b. 1927) was ordained in the Church of England in 1952 and, after curacies in London-over-the-Border, was a vicar in Romford, Essex, and the chaplain of the Barnabas Fellowship at Whatcombe House in Dorset. From 1975 until his retirement in 1992 he was county ecumenical officer of Greater Manchester. He is the author of a number of books on the charismatic renewal, pastoral liturgy and the ministry of healing, his latest being Pentecost Comes to Church: Sacraments and Spiritual Gifts *(Darton Longman and Todd 1994). He is editor of the magazine* Healing and Wholeness.

David Watson visited Manchester with a team from St Michael-le-Belfry, York, on a number of occasions in the late seventies and early eighties for his evangelistic celebrations. I was county ecumenical officer at the time and much involved in the organisation of these projects. It was on the last of these visits, sometime before he died, that David mentioned to me the name of John Wimber.

I was sitting alone with him in the Barbirolli (conductor's) room of the Free Trade Hall just before one of the evening sessions was due to begin. We were waiting for the signal to go on to the stage when David spoke warmly about a remarkable church he had visited in California and its equally remarkable pastor, John Wimber. He didn't have time to tell me much because we were summoned downstairs; but in his address that evening David related his experiences of worship in a Vineyard church and his impressions of its pastor.

As a number of contributors to this book have said, Wimber radiates an acceptance and a compassion which is the gift of a true pastor, and it was this that attracted David to him.

'John is a large, lovable, warm and gentle person, reminding me of a teddy-bear,' David wrote. 'He also has an able mind, wide Christian experience, and shrewd spiritual discernment. Every now and then in my travels I meet someone whom I feel I can really trust – someone who loves me and accepts me as I am, who is not trying to use or manipulate me, and who is full of godly wisdom. There are not many like this, but John Wimber is one.'

After David's death I heard no more of Wimber until 1985 when some friends invited me over to the meeting in Sheffield mentioned elsewhere in this book. On the stage was a group of musicians performing a series of unfamiliar rock-folksy songs. Now and then one of the musicians threw in a few remarks in a slow American voice about God and his goodness. Most of the hundreds who packed the hall seemed content to stand, some with arms outstretched, humming the tunes if they didn't know the words. But after about twenty minutes I got so bored that I sat down and wondered why I'd agreed to come. I was thinking of slipping out and waiting for my friends in the coffee-bar when the songs finished and the pianist, whom I'd hardly noticed, slowly rose from his stool, opened a Bible on the lid of the piano, and began to speak.

He wore jeans, a big belt round an ample stomach and an open-necked lumberjack's shirt. His large round face was haloed by greying hair – a Britisher's image of a trapper from the Rockies. I would not have been surprised to have seen a long rifle propped up on the other side of the piano. The voice which came over the public address system seized my attention immediately. I don't remember what he said; but he spoke for nearly an hour, and it seemed like ten minutes.

Then the ministry began – 'doin' the stuff' in Wimber jargon. He invoked the Holy Spirit and said a prayer or two. 'Words of knowledge' followed. Two or three people came up to the stage for prayer. Suddenly a woman screamed – again and again until she burst into sobbing. A rustle of anxiety swept through the hall. Immediately Wimber spoke, 'God is weeping for his church,' he explained.

At that my critical faculties went into overdrive. Ridiculous! How could anyone seriously suggest a hysterical outburst was anything other than a release of tension and nervousness? 'Weeping over the church' indeed! Was the church in Britain any worse than where this American came from? I left Sheffield in a sceptical mood, especially as one of the group I was with, a doctor, said she had not seen any healings. Yet I was intrigued enough to go to hear Wimber again the following years in Harrogate and in Birmingham.

Although neither understanding nor accepting all I heard and saw, I was nonetheless intrigued. I began to join in the Vineyard songs recognising that they provided a form of corporate contemplative worship similar to the singing of psalms to plainchant or Taizé music. I watched Wimber's clinics and on occasions copied them myself when I spoke about the ministry of healing (though in a less dramatic – and, I suspect, less effective – way). And I enjoyed his rambling biblical expositions. His dramatisation of the feeding of the five thousand is one of the funniest solo acts I have ever seen ('Bread and fish, huh? What's for afters?') I admired the way he allowed David Lewis to analyse the results of a Harrogate conference (described later); such openness is not always found among Christian leaders.

In recent years Wimber has been the subject of much study and research. He is a sitting target for post-graduate theses.

One notable instance is Martyn Percy's *Words, Wonders and Power* (SPCK, 1996), which is scholarly and objective but which I feel does not do full justice to the positive and encouraging aspects of Wimber's ministry, as Mark Stibbe points out in his contribution. So it seems an appropriate time to make a provisional assessment of the impact of Wimber's ministry on the wider church. This I have done, with the help of the publishers, by inviting church leaders of different denominations working in a variety of pastoral situations to describe what meeting Wimber has meant to them.

Reading their contributions, two things have struck me.

The first is that they all have a sincere thankfulness to God that they have met John Wimber and learned much from him. They have done this without in any sense making themselves appear as a Wimber fan club. Some of them have reservations about his teaching and practice. But if there are things they questioned or rejected, that did not prevent them from picking and mixing what was useful to them. They filtered his teaching through what they already believed as Anglicans, Baptists, Methodists, New Churches, Roman Catholics, and so on, and they adapted his practice to their own pastoral situations. They took ideas, inspirations and even visions away with them after meeting him and applied them fruitfully in their own ministries.

The second is that different individuals were encouraged in different ways. Charles Whitehead sees Wimber as a fresh breath for a renewal of the charismatic movement; John Holmes applied Wimber's practice to the ministry of healing in his church in Leeds; Chris Woods found Wimber's stress on the power of the Holy Spirit as the means of bringing an awareness of Jesus Christ to the people of his urban priority area parish in St Helens; Peter Lawrence in a very different suburban setting in the south of England; Graham Horsley found his personal ministry renewed; John Leach incorporated elements from the Vineyard style of worship into the liturgy of his church.

David Pytches, who has sponsored Wimber's visits to Britain, came to see St Andrew's, Chorleywood, as a resource for the wider church and initiated day conferences for church leaders, the New Wine holiday conferences in Somerset and the work among young people under the banner of 'Soul Survivor'. According to Gerald Coates, the New Churches were jolted into rethinking their pastoral strategy with broader experiences of the gifts of the Spirit and of power evangelism. Chris Lane represents those who believed they could only follow the Lord by leaving the denominational structures and becoming part of the Vineyard network – with a remarkable degree of success.

In telling their stories the contributors occasionally refer to events in John Wimber's life, so for those who are not familiar with his career I had better sketch this as a background to what they have written.

John Wimber was born in the American midwest in 1934. He was an only child. His father left his mother about the time of his birth, so she had to bring him up as a single parent for seven years before she married again. In the absence of a father, Wimber's grandfather – a trainer of horses – played an important part in his early life. He refers affectionately to him in his talks and books. No one in his family was a Christian. He was, as he says, 'a fourth generation unbeliever'. This caused him problems later in life when he wrestled with doubts about his Christian faith. Was he truly seeking a heavenly Father, he wondered, or was he unconsciously seeking the earthly father whom he had never known?

His family moved to California. There Wimber became absorbed in music. He learned to play the saxophone at school, and then several other instruments. From his teenage years he was a member of various local jazz bands in Orange County where he lived. His skill in teaching, directing, orchestrating and recording music made him a rich man. At the peak of his musical career he formed a group in Las

Vegas called 'The Righteous Brothers' which topped the charts.

He married Carol, a non-practising Roman Catholic, in 1955. But after a few years the marriage ran into difficulties. Shortly before the birth of their third child in 1962 the couple separated for some months, and it looked as if they would eventually be divorced. It was in the midst of this crisis that Wimber had what he calls his 'desert experience'. One morning he drove out of Las Vegas alone into the desert to watch the sun rise. As he sat in the car, reflecting on his situation, he grew more and more despondent, and in desperation uttered a prayer for God's help. When he got back to the hotel, he learned to his astonishment that his wife had phoned. In a long conversation over the phone they agreed to give their marriage another chance. It was the first time in his life that Wimber had experienced an answer to prayer.

Their marriage had been arranged with a Baptist minister whose name they had picked at random out of a telephone book, and Carol felt that they should make a fresh start by having their union blessed in a Roman Catholic church.

Dubiously Wimber agreed. Their 'remarriage' was one of the few occasions when he had been inside a church before his conversion. It was not a happy experience. He knew nothing of Christianity, and the service was incomprehensible to him, though it provided him with vivid illustrations on how *not* to conduct worship in later years!

But Wimber was still spiritually hungry. He was challenged when he heard that Dick Hind, a stand-in drummer for The Righteous Brothers, had been converted. He met others whose Christian character impressed him. This led him with Carol to join the Yorba Linda Friends' Church where his brother-in-law, Bob Fulton, was already an assistant pastor. Although the church had a Quaker tradition, it was in character an independent evangelical congregation. Through its fellowship John and Carol began to take the demands of Christian discipleship seriously. Wimber gave up his musical career and with his wife became involved in a ministry of personal evangelism. He took a course in theology at Azusa Pacific University, a Pentecostal foundation. Becoming an assistant pastor, he saw the church grow from 200 to 800 members.

The pastoral problems created by this congregational expansion led Wimber to consult Peter Wagner, a former missionary from Bolivia who was an expert in church growth and on the staff of the Fuller Theological Seminary. Wagner suggested he joined a course on evangelism and then, realising that his pupil already had considerable experience as an evangelist (he wrote later that God had taken Wimber's natural abilities as a salesman and converted them into the gift of presenting the gospel) he invited Wimber to become the founding director of the Department of Church Growth in the Institute of Evangelism and Church Growth which the seminary was setting up. So Wimber became a church consultant.

During the years he worked for the department (1974–78) Wimber travelled extensively across North America, visiting many different kinds of churches. Through seminars and consultations he taught the principles of church growth, and he became something of an expert in helping congregations to apply the theories to their own situations.

While Wimber was at Fuller, Carol, Bob Fulton and his wife, Penny, Carl Tuttle, Blain and Becky Cook and some others were baptised in the Holy Spirit. This disturbed the main body of believers in the Quaker church and they were asked to leave. As a result they began to meet in their homes. Eventually Wimber was drawn into the group and he accepted – with much reluctance – the role of chief pastor.

When Wimber assumed pastoral responsibility for the group it had about thirty members, but under his leadership that number increased rapidly. After being linked for a short time with another church, it was decided they should meet on their own, and they hired the gymnasium of Canyon High

School in the Anaheim Hills for their Sunday worship. To all appearances they were typical of many independent evangelical churches except that the music they used in their worship was largely contemporary. Wimber encouraged the members of the music group to write their own songs. They later adopted the title of the Vineyard Christian Fellowship.

His account of those first months in the pastorate is one of Wimber's amusing stories (no doubt coloured in the telling!). He relates how in his sermons he carefully expounded the Gospel of Luke, and as a result found himself having to explain the accounts of Christ's many healings. He was surprised – and alarmed – when he discovered that, as a result of his sermons, members of the congregation were beginning to pray with one another for healing.

He felt nudged by the Lord to introduce 'altar calls' into the services, and persisted in these without one person being healed. It was a difficult period. People who disagreed with the policy left the church. He was puzzled and hurt. By the end of the year he was wondering if accepting the pastorate had been a mistake. Then, one morning, ten months after he had taken charge of the congregation, one of the new members asked Wimber to come to his home and pray for the healing of his wife. With a sinking heart Wimber went to the man's house to find the wife in bed with a severe fever. In a diffident manner he placed his hands on her head, mumbled a prayer, and turned to the husband to explain why people are not healed. While he was offering his explanation – one he had offered many times before – he noticed that the husband was not listening but looking over his shoulder and grinning. Turning round, Wimber was astonished to see the wife was out of bed, looking perfectly healthy.

'What's happened to you?' he asked. 'I'm well,' she said. 'You healed me. Would you like to stay for some coffee or breakfast?' Wimber concludes his story:

'I could not believe it. She was well! I politely declined

her offer of hospitality and left. Half-way back in my car, I fully realised what had happened. All the months of questioning and despair, excitement and disappointment, revelation and humiliation – all the force of these emotions and hopes washed over me. Then I became euphoric and giddy. And I yelled at the top of my lungs, "We've got one!"'

From that time the Vineyard began to witness more healings, and this led him to realise that the relationship between gifts of healing and evangelism which was so clear in Jesus' ministry was valid still. It was out of this experience that his controversial concept of 'power evangelism' developed.

Although the Vineyard church occupied much of his time, Wimber still kept in touch with the Fuller Theological Seminary, and in 1981 he suggested to Wagner that he brought a small group from the Vineyard to lead weekly classes on what he was learning. This was the origin of the famous MC510 course on 'Signs, Wonders and Church Growth', which attracted much attention in evangelical-charismatic circles in the USA. The syllabus was seductively challenging:

'When God appears in the midst of a group of people who are yielding themselves to him and waiting for his visitation, he generally does what he does best . . . the unusual, the unexpected, the supernatural. Are you ready?

'We all "know" that God is sovereign and as such is completely free of restraints. He is free to do as he chooses. Yet learning to live in close proximity to the God of the miraculous is a process. It takes time . . .

'In few places is this progressive nature of Christian growth more clearly seen than in the area of understanding and accepting the power of the Holy Spirit in the world today.

'Becoming intimately acquainted with the Holy Spirit is vital for those who desire to pray effectively for healing. If you have not yet experienced the empowering work of the Holy Spirit, be advised that such an experience awaits you as

you move towards a healing ministry. This promised empowering is essential for service in the realm of the Spirit . . .

'This teaching is not for unbelievers or for sceptics who
must be convinced out of their scepticism. It is for believers
who want to be helped beyond the limits of their own little-
ness of faith. Your attitude is vitally important. What we do
is designed to help you move from belief to belief. It will
help you grow "from faith to faith". You will see, if you
desire to, that healing is biblical, it is for today, and it is for
you.'

Not surprisingly, the course was oversubscribed. It was
taught on successive Monday nights throughout the term.
Each session lasted three hours, and during that time Wimber
lectured on such topics as the kingdom of God, the biblical
records of the miraculous, the worldviews which Christian
theologians and preachers have which affect their interpreta-
tions of the biblical records (and, as a consequence, their
expectation of what God might – or might not – do today),
case studies of the miraculous, spiritual gifts, contemporary
faith healers, and the relationship between modern evangelism and evangelism in the power of the Holy Spirit with
signs and wonders following. These lectures formed the basis
of Wimber's later books and conference notes.

After the lecture came the 'clinic'. He involved his students in a practical way to test out what they had been
learning. He said a prayer invoking the Holy Spirit and
then sat in the front row of the class while two members of
his congregation went to the front and invited individuals to
come forward for ministry. As they prayed and laid hands on
people, Wimber quietly commented on the proceedings for
the benefit of the rest of the students. Gradually others in the
class began to join in with words of knowledge and prayer.
Sometimes they would break into smaller prayer groups.

Many received emotional or spiritual healing. Some were
healed physically. Others for the first time laid hands on a
sick person and saw him or her healed. News of what was

happening spread. The following year *Christian Life* devoted a whole issue to Wimber's teaching and course. Invitations to take teams to other cities in North America and then to other countries followed – including David Pytches' invitation to John Wimber to spend a weekend at St Andrew's, Chorley-wood, described in the next chapter. So the seeds of MC510 blew across the world.

Wimber's teaching has developed since those days. He and his team have learned much about the nature of the church and the other Christian spiritualities. He has become the focus for a worldwide network of Vineyard churches. He has experienced physical suffering in his own life and in his family and this has led him to say more about the Cross in the Christian life. At a meeting a few years ago he said with typical openness, 'I've looked death in the face and I can tell you – she ain't pretty!' And he's had to listen to much criticism and misunderstanding – from the controversy which MC510 caused at Fuller and the rumours about his ministry to David Watson in the last weeks of David's life, down to more recent events connected with Paul Cain prophecies and the 'Toronto blessing'.

These matters are discussed by the contributors in this book, and in the final chapter Martin Robinson of the Bible Society sets the Wimber phenomenon against the background of the Pentecostal and charismatic renewals and the emergence of what has been called postmodernity in the church. I will add that for me it is Wimber's gift as a church consultant which I value most.

I realised this one afternoon a few years ago at an informal meeting for church leaders in Manchester. About two hundred and fifty clergy filled the Lesser Free Trade Hall, and Wimber sat on the stage with a microphone answering their questions. Some raised problems in their pastoral work. Some criticised various aspects of his teachings. And many sought his opinion on a variety of subjects. The comments Wimber made demonstrated a wisdom, a discernment and a humility which I have rarely encountered before. I don't think anyone came away from that session without feeling they had been enlightened, affirmed, and encouraged. Whatever else may be said for or against Wimber's ministry, that afternoon will remain in my memory as a learning experience for which I shall always praise God.

CHAPTER TWO

David Pytches

*David Pytches was born in a clerical family – his father was
a Church of England Rector in Suffolk for forty years. David
was ordained in 1955 and served title at St Ebbe's, Oxford
and Holy Trinity, Wallington before going to South America
in 1959 church planting in Chile, South America, together
with Mary his wife whom he married the year before. He was
consecrated a Bishop in 1969 and was elected Bishop of the
Diocese of Chile Bolivia and Peru in 1972. He was a vicar of
St Andrew's, Chorleywood from 1977 to 1996. He has written numerous books – best known* Come Holy Spirit *and
hosted the New Wine Conferences at the Bath and West
Showground for many years.*

'Wait: I just want to back-track there on that last statement.
That wasn't the Lord – that was me.'

We were sitting in the lounge of St Andrew's and my new
friend, John Wimber, was briefing the other twenty-nine on
his team who had flown in with him from Los Angeles. It was
1981, the weekend of Pentecost, though I was not sure
whether these Vineyard folk really knew where Pentecost
fell in the Christian year. On the other hand, they were

probably wondering whether *we* knew what Pentecost was all about!

I was immediately impressed on hearing John retract his remarks. He had just – very reasonably I thought – suggested to these young people (the men among them sitting slightly uneasily in their freshly-bought English jackets with leathered elbows) that they should moderate their ministry in deference to their British host church. Obviously, this man was not concerned about being seen as a strong infallible leader. We were about to have an unforgettable weekend with these Californians, who were en route for St Michael-le-Belfry in York as guests of the late David Watson.

It was Eddie Gibbs who first introduced David Watson to John Wimber. Eddie and I had worked together in Chile for a few years, and back in the UK, when he joined the staff of the Bible Society, he had moved to Chorleywood to worship with us at St Andrew's. Whilst pursuing his Church Growth studies with the Bible Society, Eddie embarked on a doctoral course at the Fuller Theological Seminary in California and was able to visit a number of large fast-growing churches. In the process he met John Wimber and, knowing that David Watson lectured every year at Fuller, Eddie suggested to David that he should look up John Wimber. David did just that and wrote to Eddie afterwards that his ministry would never be the same again. I had great respect for David because he was a leader of renewal amongst Anglicans and was working its lessons out in a church where people could see renewal being modelled at the ground level. So when I heard that David had invited John to visit York, I wrote at once to ask John to come to Chorleywood which he did.

Several things stand out in my memory about that first visit. One was the remarkable physical manifestations of the power of the Holy Spirit. Another was the ordinariness of these people whom God was so evidently using. Yet another was the variety of results. There was the miracle of conversions – one man who is now my son-in-law being numbered among them. There were some amazing healings.

An elderly lady came up for prayer wanting sight back in her right eye. The American who prayed for her thought she said she had arthritis on her right side and was himself bowled over when she received her sight back. He had to quickly leave the church and sit quietly on a grassy bank outside whilst he recovered his breath. I was astonished to think this sort of thing could actually happen in an Anglican church. Her healing lasted to the end of her life some six or seven years later.

There was another apparent 'healing'. A lady who had been chairbound for twenty years with MS was able to get up out of her chair and wheel her husband round the church. John Wimber said at the time, 'That's a healing – not a miracle – that will need a lot more prayer.' We didn't understand the difference at the time, and neither did we have a dedicated team available to go in and keep praying. Although the lady concerned was able with company to walk down to the shops the next day, she was soon back in her chair – and died unhealed ten years later. It was perplexing indeed.

There were many other healings from that visit. Like the two examples given, some lasted and some did not. In the course of the years since, our experience has been that some have been miraculously and instantly healed, some have experienced a delayed healing, which has occurred soon after prayer, some have experienced a partial healing and they have been encouraged to come back for more. But there have been other cases of people we would have thought humanly speaking were 'most deserving' of healing who have not been healed at all – so far.

But the most significant result as far as I was concerned was that I had just seen modelled before me a missing link in the ministry of our so-called charismatic church. John Wimber had somehow discovered how to equip and activate these ordinary people for the work of the ministry.

At Wimber's final meeting, the team member who was leading called for all those with tingling, burning, heavy or shaking hands to come forward. (This, of course, is not the only sign of someone being called into a healing ministry – nor even a conclusive one – but that's how things started for us). The man then addressed me rather loudly, 'Pastor, have you got any oil?' I was embarrassed that we had none readily available in the church. I wasn't too sure about any being available in the vicarage either, but I hurried off in search. In the end, I grabbed a bottle of vegetable cooking oil from the kitchen and, pouring some into a little cut glass bowl, I picked up a clean white serviette which I folded neatly over my forearm and proceeded back into the church, handing it over with a suitable nod. After all, we Anglicans like things done decently and in order and perhaps we could leave our American friends with one or two good impressions of our Anglican church.

Seemingly oblivious of my ritual bow, my new friend grasped the bowl and began to slosh oil liberally on the hands of those lined up before him. 'Anointed for healing in the name of the Lord, Anointed for healing in the name of the Lord, Anointed . . . , Anointed . . . ,' he went down the line of about twenty people.

'Help!' was my first prayer. 'How on earth will we cope with a healing team that big? Wherever would we find enough sick people for them all to heal?'

Hoping for an answer to these problems, we called for a week of early morning prayer meetings. Then we met on the final Saturday to discuss what we thought the Lord was saying to us. Our conclusion was that since the Lord confirmed his word by the signs that accompanied the preaching of the gospel (Mark 16:20), we would offer prayer after the blessing at every major service at St Andrew's. Barry Kissell, our one-time curate, who now directed a Faith Sharing Ministry team out of St Andrew's, would also include such ministry at gatherings where they were being invited across the country.

Wimber had taught that when healing came, it would sometimes be spontaneous, sometimes be delayed, sometimes be partial. The hurting person would know it and the medical profession should be able to confirm it – at least, nearly always. I remember meeting an architect who had been healed of MS through John Wimber's ministry. After five years he visited his doctor to get a clear pronouncement of his healing. The doctor had him subjected to various tests and found no symptoms left, so my friend was bold enough to ask him, 'So I'm healed?'

'No, you are never healed of MS.'

'But I don't have any symptoms at all.'

'No,' said the doctor, 'none at all.'

'That's all right then,' said the architect. 'I don't mind having MS if I haven't got any symptoms!'

Wimber insisted we should never tell anyone to stop taking their medicine or that he or she was healed. It was strange therefore to read in David Watson's own book *Fear No Evil* (Hodder & Stoughton, 1984) that, after John Wimber and others had flown over especially to pray for him as he was dying of cancer, David believed Wimber had said he was healed. In fact, Wimber had encouraged him by saying, 'Well, I believe we've done all that we were meant to do.' David may have understood him to say, 'You're healed', but I think that is very unlikely, knowing how strongly Wimber felt about never saying such things. I later checked this with Anne Watson, David's wife, and she confirmed that she never understood him to say David was healed.

Douglas McBain, a Baptist leader in renewal at the time, organised a large conference for John Wimber in the Methodist Central Hall, London, in 1984. This brought further blessing, attracting leaders from across Britain and all over Europe. Wimber left England after this feeling that he had completed the task God had given him and that there was no call to return again. But I felt that his ministry had reached a point in this country where things were only just beginning and that it was vital he should return. So we began to plan for a visit the next year to encompass London (Wembley), Sheffield and Brighton – the latter organised by Nigel Ring from the New Frontiers church. One reason for urging Wimber to return, was a complaint from John Marsh (now Archdeacon of Blackburn) that we in the South never considered the needs of the churches further north. Hence the plan to visit Sheffield where John was a senior curate working with Canon Robert Warren, who oversaw the organisation in Sheffield and whose church, Sir Thomas' Crookes, soon became a significant centre for leaders in renewal for the Midlands and the North.

As we got organised, the need for further teaching became obvious. Mary (my wife) and I had picked up some useful material during our return visit to Anaheim. We always felt very honoured to be the guests of John and Carol Wimber. John is quite a private person and enjoys his privacy. His family frequently called over, either gathering round the swimming pool or for a meal. The Wimber home was a large, cool, wood-tiled bungalow which John had bought when he was still in the music business. It remained his home till recently when his daughter and son-in-law bought it from him and John acquired a smaller place, still in Orange County, with two bedrooms and a lakeside retreat house two hours' journey up the mountains.

In his early days we would eat out for most meals, as many Americans do – John always seemed to have some interesting Christian leaders who would meet for business lunches. Latterly the Wimbers have started to have their meals at home much more on a tasty, but simpler, diet provided by Carol. We usually ate at a large round table by the corner window with a view over their 'yard', as the Americans call their back gardens. John would relax watching golf on TV and usually went to bed at about 9.00 pm. Often he was up early to play golf with one of his family or member of staff. I was interested in the way he would encourage his grandchildren by assuming ignorance on certain things and asking them to do some research for him. For example: 'How do we get rain?' or 'How do planes keep up in the air?'

During our first visit John asked us if we would like to join him for a staff meeting. I was delighted, hoping I could improve on the way we ran ours. The team seemed to drift in about 10 am, went to the kitchen to get drinks – always with plenty of ice from the ice box – and kicked off their shoes as they sat around to chat. I was reaching in my pocket to make sure I had a pen to take notes, when suddenly in response to some signal, everyone headed out to a small white coach which whisked us away. Where? I kept wondering. Eventually we came to a seaside resort. After lunch we had a long walk by the sea, chatting to each other until we finally reboarded the coach for the return journey. It was 4 pm and the staff meeting appeared to be over. As soon as everyone had gone I asked John what had happened to the staff meeting.

'That was it.'

'Oh' I said, trying to look as though I understood.

'Staff meetings,' he said, 'are for relationship and communication. We talk business with the leaders of the different departments individually. We don't have any committees in the Vineyard.'

I had tried to persuade John to put his teaching on equipping the saints into a book. He declined. He said he was on a learning curve and might well have changed his mind on some things in six months' time. I admired his openness and humility but still insisted we must have such a book. He replied that if I felt so strongly I ought to write it myself. He offered the use of any of his material that we wanted. Combining this with our own findings at St Andrew's, Chorleywood, *Come Holy Spirit* (Hodder & Stoughton, 1985) soon appeared. This became a textbook for the teaching programme with our growing ministry team in Chorleywood. Our training sessions were opened up to the wider church – a practice we have continued over ten years or more.

Not long after the book had been published I was invited to speak at the Anglican Renewal Ministries conference at Swanwick, organised by the Director, Lawrence Hoyle. For a couple of years following this he invited Barry and me to take over the whole conference for inside the week. Eventually we began our own Swanwick conference, which we continued for two more years. We invested any profits from this into Kingdom Power Trust, which we had formed with some money donated to us by John Wimber (we have since learned of John's quiet generosity to many other causes).

We soon came to realise that the main problem for Anglican clergy attending our conferences was that there was often little support for change back in their parishes. We conceived a strategy for a longer residential conference called New Wine, which would cater for church families, so that clergy and lay leaders could come with their own local church, and together could work for change when they returned home.

In these conferences we sought to incorporate many of the values imparted to us by John Wimber, which were so much appreciated by Anglicans. These were especially reflected at the main evening meetings. There was plenty of time for worship, using a number of 'rock' songs in succession without any introductory comment. Some were joyful and praiseworthy, some tender and intimate. They were usually addressed directly to the Lord, rather than to each other about the Lord. This was followed by a teaching time based on the Word of God. The speaker was simply introduced without razzmatazz – trying always not to take the focus off the Lord. For the same reason we kept advertising and public prayer requests to an absolute minimum. Finally there was plenty of time for prayer ministry to individuals wanting it after the worship and teaching. The conferences also offered a variety of workshops, led by people known to be good communicators and effective on their subject.

In spite of reports to the contrary, New Wine (out of which two Soul Survivor conferences for youth and the Lakeside

Conference have also developed) was never organised by or the responsibility of the Vineyard Ministries International, though it was Wimber who had encouraged us to start this. We have had many Vineyard speakers and a number of their music leaders to help us with our worship. The first year, 1989, at the Royal Bath and West Showground we had three-and-a-half thousand. Every year since that first August in Somerset the numbers have grown. In 1995, when John Wimber came over to give the main Bible readings, we had seven-and-a-half thousand at New Wine, a thousand more in an 'overflow' conference called 'Lakeside' the previous week and two Soul Survivor conferences with about three-and-a-half thousand young people at each. 80% of those attending are from the Church of England, including Episcopalians who have flown over to join us from the USA and Anglicans who have come from Canada. Latterly the New Wine conference has been almost fully booked by the end of January each year.

We chose the Royal Bath and West Showground because it seemed to offer the best price and facilities and was available at the right time. Elm House had been holding their conference there for several years, but were now packing up. They were wonderfully kind to us in helping us to get started. Looking back, I think they must have been quite concerned for us, wondering what on earth did we think we could do with so little experience and so few clues about running a large family conference.

The mention of Bible readings reminds me that my earliest and most favourable impressions concern John Wimber's great ability to expound the Scriptures. Anyone who has seen John Wimber's personal library will know how widely read he is. He has a great ability to memorise the main argument of a book, over which he reflects deeply before imparting it to others in a very lucid manner. John is always trying to hear God and admits he has often heard the Lord speak through his wife Carol (a one-time Roman

Catholic from a large family; her father was a physician). She is often surprised at the way John will include in his teaching an insight of her own, which she had never even imagined John had taken seriously at the time.

During the eighteen years of the Vineyard's existence at Anaheim John has worked systematically through some thirty-six books of the Bible. He expounds a biblical theology of suffering (he has himself experienced suffering with cancer, as has his eldest son). He also teaches a biblical theology of healing and of responsibility to the poor. The Anaheim Vineyard regularly gives away $50,000 plus a month (and one Sunday recently $750,000) to feed the poor, something many of those who have ignorantly criticised Wimber for not doing would find it difficult to match. His teaching is always delivered in a very natural laid-back style, illustrated from a wealth of experience and wide reading. John is a gifted evangelist, a church planter and a church consultant, as well now as being the 'archbishop' for a large and growing number of Vineyards around the world. The first Vineyard in Britain was founded in 1987 and there are now twenty-five. Four of the first leaders came from the Church of England, where they had been ordained. Today there are over 700 Vineyards in the world, spread across thirty nations.

It is important to stress this because John has come to be regarded abroad as the 'signs and wonders' man. His very effective all-round ministry is often ignored. Another element in his widespread popularity has been his genuine love for the whole church right across all the denominations. He has also consistently eschewed taking up specific lines on such matters as eschatology, the doctrine of the last things, on which so many Christians have sadly been divided. He believes this distracts from the things clearly taught by Scripture. 'The plain thing is the main thing and the main thing is the plain thing' is a favourite saying of his. He has a simple desire to extend the Kingdom of God through evangelism, church growth and church planting and to use all the resources that God has provided to equip his church through the Holy Spirit. John has not veered from his original focus on 'the Blood' and 'the Book' – the Cross of Christ and the Bible. His values are worship and compassion.

During the course of his ministry John Wimber has been subject to the most extraordinary slander on the air and libel in print. Several times I have seen him brush aside articles which people have thoughtfully written and offered to publish in his defence. 'No,' he would say, 'we don't want to get into that. That's only playing them at their own game.' He would never defend himself. At one time only he allowed some of his defenders to publish answers to his critics, and that was not because John wanted this for himself, but because the Vineyard leadership in general felt it was important to produce an authentic *apologia pro vita sua* for the sake of the whole movement.

About 1988 or 1989 John had arranged to stay with us in Chorleywood after leading a conference in Scotland. He asked whether he might bring a fellow conference speaker, whom he thought we would be interested to meet. In due time John arrived with Mike Bickle from Kansas City. Mike told us how his church had been planted and grown through significant 'words' given him by prophets. I believed that prophecy was a gift of the Holy Spirit available to the church today and had attended a School of Prophecy at Anaheim organised by Wimber to learn more about it. We had tried for many years to encourage prophecy in St Andrew's, but in general, whilst not wanting to despise it, it seemed that much of this was simply blessed thoughts. Now here was a man who had prophetic people around him, who were clearly receiving significant revelation from God.

Since we were ourselves soon off to the USA for a series of conferences in Episcopal churches, we arranged to fit in a visit to Kansas City to meet these prophetic people. I followed this up with a little book called *Some Said It Thundered* (Hodder & Stoughton, 1990). In it I spelt out some of the background stories of these prophets and described how Mike Bickle's church had developed apparently out of direct revelation from God. The book was intended to supplement the various articles which were appearing in Christian publications in the UK and, it was hoped, would prepare the ground for a conference on prophecy which Wimber was to hold in London at Holy Trinity Church, Brompton. The book's publication was greeted with some hostility, so when I was writing a later book on the subject of prophecy, Barry Kissell joked publicly that my next book following *Some Said It Thundered* would be called *Some Said It Didn't*!

The opposition became focused mainly on one of the so-called Kansas City prophets, Bob Jones. Bob had been remarkably used by God in the building up of what became known as the Kansas City Metro Vineyard under Mike Bickle's leadership. Paul Cain was introduced later to Kansas City and there were some powerful manifestations at public meetings during his visit. This was difficult for Bob who felt overshadowed and sadly fell into sin, for which he was quickly and publicly disciplined. All this was used to try to discredit the prophetic ministry emanating from the Metro Vineyard.

One of the leading charismatic pastors in Kansas City published a mountain of charges against the Metro Vineyard, its prophets and pastor. These papers were hastily circulated across Britain. John Wimber ordered a team to investigate the charges, but in the end there appeared very little of substance in them though Mike Bickle recognised that the charge of pride against him – one of the youngest pastors in town, but clearly blessed by God – was true. He acknowledged this before God and immediately repented of it publicly, both in the USA and the UK. What Mike never revealed at the time when so many false charges were circulating against him, was that he knew that their author – the leading charismatic pastor – was in fact a womaniser, who later left his own wife and church to run off with his secretary. This poor man has since repented and made peace with Mike Bickle, and the whole affair has become a matter of public knowledge in Kansas City.

It was at Kansas that I first met Paul Cain. I was impressed by his humility, dislike of the limelight, desire to keep the focus on 'Jesus Christ and him crucified' and above all, for the high level of revelation from God which he appeared to be receiving. There was considerable hostility to Paul Cain following his appearance in Britain and he was denounced as a false prophet. This, of course, was dismissed by the vast majority of Christians when they met him or heard him and were able to 'try the spirits'. No prophet is infallible. The New Testament teaches all prophecies should be tested and weighed. One of the objections to Paul Cain was that he misled 'the body evangelical' by foretelling a revival which would break out during a specific month in the early nineties and which moved John Wimber to organise a conference at the London Docklands, perhaps even to be involved in its initiation here.

It was a good conference and thousands were blessed at it, but whether there were (what Wimber later clarified as the actual words Paul had used to him) 'tokens of revival' is up to history to judge. I expressed my own views publicly at a leaders' conference in Chorleywood a few months later. I think it was possible that something began, and that a flame was lit which would later impact the country dramatically. I wonder if in future years it will be seen that in some way the Alpha movement took a significant boost at the time, or someone who will come to have a measurable role in the revival was set on fire then. We have to accept that Paul could also have been wrong, yet at the same time remember that a false prophecy does not make a false prophet. As John Wimber frequently reminded us, 'Be very humble; in all the gifts of the Spirit; you could be wrong.' Where it is God, it will authenticate itself; where it isn't, it will fall to the ground. It could also mean that Paul Cain saw clearly what was to come but as can so often happen, he got the timing wrong. Or that it was certainly God s desire, but that opposition quenched the Spirit and God changed his mind (Jeremiah 18:10).

John's ministry has brought together a number of churches which have responded to his vision and inspired the formation of great numbers of new ones. One of the Vineyard Fellowships which achieved considerable publicity was the Airport Vineyard at Toronto. Under John Arnott's leadership this church has become a major focus for spiritual refreshing for thousands of Christian leaders from all over the world, not to mention many other thousands who have found Christ there as Lord and Saviour.

The Airport Vineyard has been having nightly meetings (except Mondays) for over two years now and at least two other centres in the USA and one in the UK (Sunderland) have followed suit bringing great blessing to thousands more. These particular Fellowships have taken on a different dynamic from the average Vineyard and become revival centres. This has evidently caused some stress within the Vineyard movement itself. John Wimber has always taught, outward manifestations are not necessary or proof that one is being touched by the Holy Spirit even though there may often be such manifestations, as there certainly were at the majority of his meetings. But the response at Toronto was to have catchers behind people being ministered to and marks taped out on the floor to indicate where to fall. This appeared to contradict John's teaching and to imply that a fall was expected. Of course, where people were getting hurt through people falling on them, the Airport Fellowship had to do something. It seems to have been over a number of conflicting values such as these, that it was deemed best to separate the two movements organisationally. This is a typical American way of solving a problem – probably the product of an inherent puritan gene taken over by the original settlers, but to many Englishmen it may be mystifying and painful. For our part, we remain deeply indebted to God for John and Carol Wimber as we do for John and Carol Arnott and we want to continue to bless both and be blessed by both.

Over the years since John Wimber's first visit to us in 1981, a time of considerable disillusionment amongst the clergy and large scale drop-outs from the laity, thousands of leaders have been renewed, inspired and envisioned through the ministry of the Holy Spirit. Hundreds of students have produced theses on his message and ministry. Many have produced masters' degrees or doctorates on areas that have become revitalised largely through John's ministry, especially healing, prophecy and church planting. Indeed, it is interesting to note on a broad front how theology in general has become decidedly refocused on the Holy Trinity once again. I do not think this is a coincidence. I believe one of the major factors in this swing back to orthodoxy and the current revival in the churches may well have been the influence of John Wimber. He arrived on the scene in Britain at a critical time in the charismatic movement and he has been a major Christian instrument in encouraging the church to trust in the leading and the work of the Holy Spirit.

CHAPTER THREE

Charles Whitehead

Charles Whitehead (b. 1942) is President of ICCRS, International Catholic Charismatic Renewal Services. He has been a leader in the charismatic renewal since the late 1970s, and is a regular contributor to Christian magazines around the world. He is the author of Pentecost is for Living *(Darton, Longman & Todd 1993) which has been translated into five languages. He combines his Christian work with a business career in the paper industry, and is married to Sue. They have four children.*

Occasionally my first meeting with someone is accompanied by a sense of the importance of the moment. It doesn't happen often, so I've learned to recognise such meetings as significant in the purposes of God. I met John Wimber in 1984 when he came to London for his first conference for leaders at Westminster Central Hall. I had no idea during the worship time who the well-rounded, bearded man playing the piano was, but somehow it came as no surprise when he was introduced and called to the microphone to begin the teaching. I was immediately struck by his warmth, his superb gifts of communication, and his total lack of pomposity. My first thoughts were that this was someone I could trust, someone with whom I could work. He seemed to have a lot to teach us about the things of God and I wanted to be open to him and to learn from him.

I believe this spontaneous first assessment is as true today as it was then. So what has been the impact of this man on my own ministry and on Catholics in Britain? What have we learned through him? These are the questions I will be trying to address as honestly as I can in my chapter.

I like John Wimber – there is something warm, open, and engaging about him. He's prepared to listen, so I don't find him threatening. He's always interested in learning, so he doesn't come across as dogmatic. He has a fine sense of humour, so he's able to say challenging and difficult things without alienating anyone. He's happy to laugh at himself. He admits he doesn't have all the answers, so it's easy to identify with him. I enjoyed his description of himself as 'just a fat man trying to get to heaven', and I've had a number of fascinating and challenging conversations with him. Sue, my wife, and I greatly enjoyed working with him and his team in Poland a few years ago, and I've been impressed by the Vineyard pastors I've met. He seems to draw good people together, and for me that's a sure sign of a fine leader. But before making a more personal assessment, I'd like to look at the impact he's had on Catholics in Britain.

In the Roman Catholic church in Britain it's the charismatics who have had contact with John Wimber and the Vineyard churches. The great majority of Catholics here would not even know who he is. So what impact has he had? How significant has it been? In my view it has gone far beyond the small numbers of charismatics who have actually attended his conferences, listened to his tapes, or read his books. He's played an important part in reminding the charismatic renewal of its first call and equipping us to respond to that call.

There have been three major areas of impact: his emphasis on the importance of the gifts of the Holy Spirit; the need to equip ordinary people to minister in the power of the Spirit; and a healthy reminder that the gifts are to be used in evangelism.

To help explain the importance of these basic messages for Catholic charismatics, I hope you will bear with me while I give some background to the situation in the Catholic charismatic renewal at the beginning of the 1980s.

In 1967 the charismatic renewal burst into the life of an unsuspecting Catholic church which was still struggling to implement the changes and reforms of the recently concluded Vatican Council. From small beginnings among a handful of college students, the fire of the Holy Spirit swept through the church so that fifteen years later the Catholic charismatic renewal was to be found in every country, touching and changing the lives of millions of men and women from all walks of life. No grass-roots movement had ever travelled so far, as fast, or as powerfully as the charismatic renewal. Here in Britain prayer meetings had mushroomed all over the country, and there were new communities and ministries bringing fresh life to local churches.

But sadly by the 1980s things were beginning to slow down again. The early leaders were becoming tired. Finding it harder to step out in faith, we were beginning to rely once again on techniques and systems, and less on the Holy Spirit. There was a real danger that what had started as a mighty move of God was being continued in our human strength. The early excitement was passing and yet many of the old problems remained, so we were starting to build a theology around our unbelief, explaining why God would probably *not* act. We were slipping back into the safety of structure and ritual, trying to reform ourselves and society by our natural energy. We even wondered if the Holy Spirit was withdrawing his gifts – a fear which easily leads to paralysis and inactivity. Where would the charismatic renewal be if it no longer exercised the charisms, the gifts of the Holy Spirit?

At the same time many of our charismatic groups were

becoming cosy little clubs – holy huddles for like-minded people. The call to evangelise which stands so clearly at the heart of the gospel was being largely ignored. The enthusiasm to spread the message of new life in the Holy Spirit which had characterised the early years of the charismatic renewal was missing. We were in danger of forgetting that the church exists to evangelise. Into this situation in Britain came a man sent by God. His name was John – John Wimber.

Wimber's contribution to the Catholic charismatic renewal in Britain was to focus our attention again on the importance of the gifts of the Spirit, to remind us how to use them, and to equip us to go out and evangelise others in the power of the Holy Spirit. The Wimber method of teaching, demonstrating, and then experiencing, broke through the unwillingness to trust God which was beginning to paralyse some of our ministry. He made the supernatural power of God seem normal – something we should confidently expect God to release when we called upon him. His practical, down-to-earth approach was both refreshing and invigorating. His style of teaching made his message accessible to everyone, and his own confidence in God was infectious. There's no doubt in my mind that John Wimber's visits to Britain in the 1980s had a major impact on a number of key leaders in the Catholic charismatic renewal at a time when it would have been easy to slip back into a much more conservative approach to the gifts of the Holy Spirit.

Perhaps of even greater significance was his emphasis on body ministry – the equipping of almost everyone to exercise their gifts for the benefit of the whole body. At local level in the Catholic church there is always a great danger that we have an over-emphasis on the leader. This results in the shrinking of most ministry into the hands of one person – the priest. As a result priority is given to liturgy and maintenance rather than to teaching, evangelisation, and individual pastoral care. The laity often see themselves as spectators, with the priest the only important player in the game. In fact, he is supposed to be the team coach motivating, directing, inspiring, and training his team. It's a question of partnership – we're all in this together and we need to play our full part.

In the charismatic renewal the most gifted leaders were often expected to exercise the gifts for the benefit of everyone else, and so ministry was still in the hands of only a few special people. John Wimber's emphasis on equipping everyone for ministry spoke directly into this situation with important results. Of course, the ensuing surge of life and evangelistic zeal put pressure on our structures and systems, demanding a change in attitude among some of our leaders. But this was all to the good. Wherever Wimber went people returned to their groups and churches with an unshakeable conviction that they should be allowed to use their gifts for the benefit of the whole body.

When it came to the call to go out and evangelise, which accompanied all Wimber's teaching supported by testimonies from team members, the message was also timely and significant. Evangelisation was something with which most Catholics were neither familiar nor comfortable. It had always been looked upon as a job for the specialists – priests, nuns, and missionaries. The truth that it is something to which every Christian is called through baptism had gone unnoticed by the vast majority. An over-stretched priesthood had seen its primary task as maintenance rather than mission, and an unquestioning laity had accepted that to live a good Christian life they just needed to 'keep' the faith.

Voices were already being raised to correct the situation, but Wimber's contribution was to highlight the use of the gifts in evangelisation. This clearly showed that charismatics had something special to bring to the party – despite the fact that this made others even more nervous of the whole idea! It was easy to support the teaching with solid scriptural evidence from the New Testament, and Wimber's message sat comfortably with the New Evangelisation call of Pope John Paul II.

One of the interesting things about John Wimber and his ministry is that he's acceptable to different types of Christians. He's acceptable to many evangelicals because his teaching on the supernatural has a clear biblical base, and he encourages a rational, thinking approach. He's acceptable to charismatics because of his total commitment to the exercise of the supernatural power of God in the healing ministry. And he's acceptable to Catholics because of his emphasis on worship, his openness to the mystical and his desire for unity.

Having said all this, I need to emphasise that the impact John Wimber's teaching had was on a relatively small number of charismatic leaders, and that the vast majority of Catholics in Britain were totally unaware of his existence. Nevertheless, those who went to hear him came away greatly encouraged and determined to put into practice what they had previously known in their hearts but had now experienced. Wimber's high profile in charismatic circles and his exceptionally effective gifts of communication and motivation resulted in an impact that went far beyond the small numbers who actually experienced his teaching and ministry first hand.

What was *not* so good was that some of the people who went to Wimber's conferences to be equipped for ministry were the very people the local leaders were anxious to restrain. I well remember my own heart sinking at the sight of a 'Wimberised' man striding forward to minister with shining eyes and twitching hands – a man I knew to be totally without either discernment or even common sense. Many returned to their local groups convinced they had a right to be confirmed in a prophetic ministry of healing and deliverance, just because they had attended a Wimber conference. But perhaps this was a small price to pay for the many excellent men and women who found a new enthusiasm and a new confidence through their contact with John Wimber and his teams in the 1980s.

What of my own experience of John and his teaching? I've already said that I like him and given some of my reasons, but there's more to it than that. I hold many of the same convictions.

- I'm convinced of the supreme importance of unity in the body of Christ, and by that I don't mean uniformity where we all do everything the same way. There's a richness in diversity, but we need to be open to one another and to recognise that in spite of many deeply-held beliefs that separate us there *is* a fundamental unity in Christ. So we need to be prepared to talk to each other, to worship the Lord together, and wherever possible to cooperate. I know there's often a price to be paid for this, and that John Wimber has paid the price for cooperating with Catholics. Without knowing it, he has strengthened my conviction that it's always worth paying the price for unity.

- I'm convinced, too, that we need men and women of courage, who are willing to be associated with people and ministries which sometimes cause controversy and disagreement. So I believe Wimber was right to use his high profile to raise the prophetic as an important ministry, even though it was bound to be controversial and to cause him problems. In my own experience the ministry of Paul Cain in particular has been a great blessing to many of us, and we have Wimber to thank for bringing him to our notice.

- I share John Wimber's conviction about the centrality of worship in all that we do, and I find the Vineyard style of worship attractive. Where some complain that it's repetitive, I find the repetition of truth liberating; where others may say that the words are simplistic, I *want* to be child-like before the Father; whilst there are those who prefer a more vigorous style, I appreciate the still small voice and the gentle breeze. We have been blessed by introducing Vineyard songs into our times of worship.

- I know how important communication is, particularly the avoidance of jargon. Wimber's account of his first visit to a church service convinced me that I must be constantly vigilant and avoid using 'churchy' language – all it does is obscure our message. I share his conviction that humour and example carry home the message better than anything else.

- I admire John Wimber's determination to avoid fruitless debate and argument. On one occasion I remember listening to someone exhorting John to defend himself against some false accusations – it was suggested that he should write an article making his position clear. He refused, saying that people could make up their own minds based on what he was saying and teaching. To get into public arguments was not honouring to God.

- I tend to take a pragmatic approach to many things, to go along with what seems to work. Wimber's approach is often the same. Sometimes we need to go with what God seems to be doing even when we don't fully understand it and can't immediately explain it. This approach often brings criticism, but although there are risks and we may be wrong it means we allow God the freedom to do new things.

- I respect people who persevere when nothing seems to be happening just because they are sure they are doing God's will, and I have enjoyed Wimber's accounts of his early attempts in the ministry of healing. Most people he prayed for got worse and some died – but he persevered and one day the breakthrough came. Perseverance in prayer and ministry would transform the lives of many of us.

Of course, there have been disappointments too. Wimber is the first to admit he has made mistakes. A few things have caused me concern – the conviction that David Watson would live, the claims of some healings that proved incorrect, the promotion of *some* of the Kansas City prophets, the prophecies about a great revival starting in England, and most recently the break with the now renamed Toronto Airport Christian Fellowship. Surely this one could have been avoided with better communication? Similar types of division have occurred so often in the past, so could not a man of Wimber's gifts and experience have done it differently this time? Ten years ago I think it would have been different, but age makes all of us more conservative, less comfortable on the cutting edge and more prepared to listen to the voices of caution around us. I've read the exchanges between John Arnott and John Wimber with great sadness, even though both men retain an honest desire for the best for each other. But all these disappointments do not significantly detract from the contribution John Wimber has made to the charismatic churches in the United Kingdom. Because of his faithfulness in answering God's call to minister frequently over here, new life has flowed into our groups, fellowships, and churches. For that we owe him a debt of gratitude.

In concluding, I recognise that I have not had as much personal contact with John Wimber as some who have contributed chapters to this book. I do not profess to be as well-qualified theologically or as experienced pastorally as others. In fact I have much more experience of sitting at Wimber's feet to receive teaching and ministry from him than of standing with him on a platform. But from the beginning I have liked and enjoyed what I have seen, heard, read and received. I believe his impact on Catholic charismatic renewal in England in particular has been very important. It has been a timely, godly, and effective impact, and has gone far beyond the small number who have actually experienced his teaching and ministry first hand.

So I will always be grateful to this likeable, entertaining, courageous and very gifted servant of the Lord.

CHAPTER FOUR

Nigel Wright

Dr Nigel Wright (b. 1949) has been the senior pastor of Altrincham Baptist Church, Cheshire since 1995. Previously he was pastor of Ansdell Baptist Church and lecturer in Christian Doctrine at Spurgeon's College, London. He is the author of a number of books including The Radical Kingdom, The Fair Face of Evil, Challenge to Change *and* The Radical Evangelical *and co-author with Tom Smail and Andrew Walker of* Charismatic Renewal: The Search for a Theology. *He has been chair of Mainstream: Baptists for Life and Growth and serves in a variety of denominational and ecumenical roles. He is married to Judy and their children Jonathan and Hannah are at university.*

My first encounter with John Wimber was in 1982. At the time I was pastor of a Baptist church on the Lancashire coast at Ansdell, Lytham St Anne's and had been there for nine years. For four years we had been exploring the charismatic movement and had moved substantially in this direction, meeting all the characteristic problems along the way. To stimulate the work of renewal we had been holding renewal weekends, inviting a wide variety of speakers to give us the benefit of their ministry for a time. When therefore I first

45

received a phone call from those working in the church growth side of the Bible Society, it was with one of these weekends in mind that I followed it through.

In addition, the church had been influenced by the Dales Bible Week and the early stages of the Restoration movement. We were in the process of sifting through the ideas and methods associated with this grouping. By this time we had adopted a take-it-and-leave-it approach, accepting gratefully the things that we found helpful to us, but disentangling them in the process from what we considered less appropriate to ourselves or concerning which we had uneasy feelings. We were becoming increasingly an independently-minded charismatic fellowship with Baptist convictions and practices. It was into this context that John and his team arrived.

Their coming was not without some amusing aspects. To transport a group of about thirty jet-lagged Californians first to Britain and then to Lancashire makes for some cultural contrasts. We borrowed the local Pentecostal church's coach and driver in order to pick them up from Blackpool station. While driving along the Golden Mile I tried my hand as a tour-guide and explained about Blackpool, pointing out the Irish Sea in the process. Whether or not it was my accent I don't know, but I was obviously failing to communicate. Most of the team probably didn't have a clue as to where they were. However it didn't take long for the atmosphere to thaw and by the time we were back at the church things were looking up. They looked up even more once we were able to pair up the visitors with their hosts. The fragrant, gum-chewing Californians were an instant hit. Charming, affirmative and relaxed, they quickly made friends and won hearts.

With John were his wife Carol, Bob and Penny Fulton and Sam and Gloria Thompson, all close associates in the work of the Vineyard Christian Fellowship in Orange County, California. There followed a weekend which exceeded all our expectations, yet there was nothing in the build-up to the event nor in the weekend itself which in any way could be described as 'hype'. John's teaching about power evangelism was at first academic, dry and even halting, as though he had been given a brief with which he was not entirely comfortable. Only when he laid his notes aside and began to speak from the heart did things get going. This he did on the Saturday afternoon.

Those who are familiar with the Vineyard and its ministry need only imagine. He introduced a member of the party called Lonnie Frisbee whom he called their 'fun-maker'. Lonnie climbed into the pulpit and invited us to sing *Majesty* twice (these were the days before that particular song had been sung to death). Then he simply prayed, 'Come, Holy Spirit.' Within seconds the Holy Spirit fell upon those who were there. I was pushed down into my seat and then onto the floor by the weight of God's presence and found myself calling upon the name of the Lord at the top of my voice. All around me, as far as I could tell from the floor, similar things were happening. Many (men as it happened) were reeling round as though they were drunk. Lonnie was stringing them together like a daisy chain.

Strangely, inwardly I felt calm and quietly detached from it all. Californians gathered round me to pray, 'More, Lord. Give him more.' While this was happening John assumed control and began gently to explain what was going on; about waves of the Spirit coming like waves on the seashore; about what different physical phenomena might mean and how varied they were; about ministering to each other and praying in teams for each other; about all God's people being used in ministry; about healing. It was a steep learning curve.

The fact that John seemed to understand what was going on was reassuring. I certainly didn't; but it felt right. We had asked God to come and meet with us and it was happening. I had to make a split-second decision about whether this was God at work or not and decided that it must be. For the next two hours many people received prayer and a very large proportion of those present entered into experiences of the

Spirit's power beyond anything they had previously imagined. It amounted to a remarkable move of the Spirit in our congregation and was also, incidentally, hugely enjoyable.

A key ingredient in this whole episode was John Wimber's own attitude and demeanour; his patient explanations; his ability to let things happen without hyping them up; his respect for where people were and his understanding of their hesitations and fears. Beyond all this was the underlying principle that the work of ministry is not about creating anointed 'stars' but enabling all God's people to minister.

I would describe myself as by nature a sane and sober person with a fair portion of common sense. I am not easily swayed and take a cautious stance towards high-sounding claims. At the same time I am open towards others, their opinions and the possibilities of new experience. The essential factor for me in the Wimber visit was the sense that John was a person who could be trusted. This was in part because of his genial and friendly appearance and his lack of aggression towards those who criticised him, and also because of his ability to affirm other people. There is an interesting contrast here between John's style and the kind of Restorationism with which we had had contact. Restorationists of that era seemed to project an image which suggested they had discovered the right way to be the church. The essence of their new revelation was the need to be related to an apostle and to have in place in the church an authority structure based upon the dominance of male elders. The proper church was also constituted with house groups. As is typical for all religious groups, the architecture of the church's meeting place illustrated the church's style and theology. It was important, therefore, not to have pews or a pulpit and for the worship area to be as non-religious in appearance as possible. The headscarf was established as having almost sacramental significance, symbolising the submission of a wife to her husband or to the elders.

The total effect of these incidental trappings of a particular church order was to create a strong sense of the 'correct' way of being the church so that, if you did not conform to them, you were subliminally and sometimes explicitly regarded as 'non-kosher'. As a Baptist congregation which had walked some of the journey with Restorationists, it had become clear to us that we were regarded as less than fully church. We were not a 'kingdom' church because we were not submitted to an external apostle with acceptable credentials (although who legitimates such people is still not clear to me) and because we still practised the kind of democratic account-ability which is symbolised by the church meeting. The truth was that we were glad to be who and what we were.

On encountering John Wimber we met with a very different spirit from the Restorationist one. This was not a person who was out to judge whether we were acceptable or not but someone who simply accepted us for who and where we were. An early theme that John struck at this time was that God loved the whole of the church and he loved it in all its variety and with all its foibles. In place of the qualified acceptance we had experienced at the hands of Restoration-ists, which told us we were acceptable provided we kept moving in the right direction and intended to become what we should become, John's attitude and that of the team he led was one of openness to us and appreciation of us right where we were. This won our hearts and made us feel good. It was the basis on which, within a framework of trust and respect, some interesting things could happen.

There were a number of small but significant indications of this attitude. Whereas visiting Restorationists obviously regarded the organ as an instrument belonging to the old order of church life, the Wimber team loved it, especially when organ and violin played together. Whereas the high pulpit (which I hardly ever used) had been a politically-incorrect embarrassment, it suddenly came into its own as a place to stand in order to see what the Spirit was 'doing' amongst the people. For John, although matters of church order were not unimportant, the more important thing was where we were in the whole matter of knowing God and living in the power of the Spirit. We could trust a person who after such a short time treated us like this.

I was to learn in conversation with John that this openness of attitude is accompanied by a model of church which is carefully thought through and highly attractive. Churches may be placed on a spectrum which is defined at one end as a 'bounded-set' and at the other as a 'bounded-centre'. The bounded-set is the kind of church which establishes a clear boundary between those who belong and those who do not. As an example, the boundary might be created by the need to give assent to a number of doctrines or to show evidence of a range of experiences. Much attention is given to whether or not people 'belong', that is, whether they have passed the test and crossed the boundary. At the same time sight is lost of whether those within the bounded set are making further progress into the church or are on their way out of it. Bounded-set churches are strong at nurturing and teaching but because of the boundaries set around them tend not to be evangelistic. They are difficult to gain access to. By contrast bounded-centre churches have very fluid boundaries. It is not always clear who 'belongs' and who does not, but there is a central focus and people are invited to move towards what is at the centre from whatever point they are starting. There is a high degree of acceptance of people, and space is allowed for movement and development. As a consequence such churches prove effective in evangelism although they may not be as strong on the teaching side.

As what is being described here is a spectrum, most churches would find themselves at some point along it and would fully match neither the bounded-set nor bounded-centre types. Presumably the aim is to combine the strengths of both types. A Restoration-type church with a strong stress on 'commitment' and a lengthy induction process for new members fits clearly into the bounded-set type (although it should be admitted that the Restoration scene has changed over the years). An example of a bounded-centre would be a lively Anglican parish church with its requirement to be open to all in the locality. There are many examples of such churches proving evangelistically fruitful over long periods of time. The Vineyard model of the church is also of this kind. Thus an open model of the church accompanies an openness of spirit and attitude in John Wimber's own approach. To encounter both this attitude and this thinking was a breath of fresh air and indicated to us that the Wimber project consisted in far more than the stress upon signs and wonders and intimate worship.

Although Wimber is by no means a Baptist, he has proven himself able to work with others in a wide variety of churches. At the end of the day I would probably disagree with him on the best kind of ecclesiology to adopt, but at the time of his visit I was becoming increasingly aware of the need to preserve freedom within the church. Shepherding emphases were at their height in the early and mid-1980s and seemed to me to lock people into constricting relationships which could only create dependency and stultify spiritual and human freedom. Wimber showed an alternative way which had its own spiritual intensity and yet which maintained the freedom of the Christian and, as the Association of Vineyard Churches developed, allowed for the autonomy of local churches. All of this could be incorporated within a Baptist understanding of the church with its insistence upon religious liberty, freedom of conscience, the gathered church, the accountability of leaders to the congregation, and the need and responsibility for all members to be involved in the process of discerning the mind of Christ in governing the church's affairs.

Over the years there have been other areas which, while maintaining respect and affection for John and his work, have given me reason for concern and caused me to move

off in other directions. The most significant involves linger-
ing doubts both about the essential Wimber thesis that signs
and wonders are the necessary accompaniment of effective
evangelism and about the nature and value of the phenomena
with which his name has become so closely identified. It was
my experience as a pastor in a local church that in the wake
of various Vineyard visits there were more wonders than
signs. People would manifest all manner of tremblings, fall-
ings down, fluttering eyelids, prophesyings, and originally
these were understood as the power of God resting upon
people to heal them or to enable them to heal others. Yet
the outcome of all of this in terms of significant healings was
minimal.

This is a complex area because on inspection it becomes
extremely difficult to establish what would constitute clear
evidence of a healing miracle. Many people will testify to
healing, but usually this is of some complaint, minor or
otherwise, not visible to the human eye or of a form of illness
which was only tentatively diagnosed in the first place. When
it came to specific, visible and known sickness the healing
rate in response to much prayer has, in my experience, been
inconsiderable. This very fact seems to be in contradiction to
the claim that God is actively looking for opportunities to
heal the sick in order to confirm his Word. If faith the size of
a mustard seed is what is required then the conditions for
healing have been there on numerous occasions but without
result. The 'cognitive dissonance' approach to this seeks to
rationalise it by finding reasons why the healing has not
happened. But this is a road I refuse to take since it leads
to despair and treats an act of healing as though it were a
human accomplishment, achieved by our providing the right
conditions for it to happen. This is not how I understand the
gracious gifts of God. I have come to the conclusion that God
is not as interested in healing miracles and powerful acts as
we are.

There is a difference between healing in the ministry of

Jesus and our own ministry at this point. Jesus healed marginalised people in order that they might be restored to the worshipping community of Israel from which their sickness more or less excluded them. That ministry cannot be translated into a privileged Western context without changing its meaning, since the sick are not religiously excluded amongst us as they were in Israel. Neither am I persuaded that the attempt to perform acts of power adds impetus to the evangelistic task as the Wimber thesis claims. All the evidence available to me suggests that the primary ingredient in evangelism is loving relationships. The attempt to produce miracles leads more often than not to suspicion that some kind of hype is being perpetrated, as the general response to Morris Cerullo seems to suggest. In short we are side-tracked when the emphasis falls upon *power* as the means by which the gospel will be validated in our day. The gospel is validated by unconditional *love*.

From time to time such love might issue in some act of healing and restoration. The church should of course pray for the sick but not primarily in the hope of producing acts of power; rather such ministry is active demonstration of the loving care of God and his people. The defining moment for me was at a Wimber meeting at Holy Trinity, Brompton, when along with others I found myself praying with a devastatingly crippled woman suffering from Huntington's chorea. We prayed ourselves into despair. I could only guess at what the woman, unable to communicate, made of it all.

Recently the so-called 'Toronto blessing' has brought into prominence once more the kind of phenomena which accompanied the Wimber visits of the 1980s. A whole set of questions has been raised concerning the nature and value of these experiences, with many testifying to a deep work of God and others finding it impossible to square their understanding of the gospel with such oddities. I have been able to develop a theological framework which understands such phenomena as forms of response to the divine presence, a response which issues from the hidden, psychic depths of our human make-up. The phenomena are human experiences brought about by certain stimuli, but precisely because they are *human* they participate in all the ambiguities of our human nature. In other words, they may be responses to the divine but can also be provoked by other stimuli. Clearly, analogies exist for these phenomena in Scripture but an *analogy* invites us to note the dissimilarities as well as the similarities. There is a world of difference between such things happening spontaneously as infrequent occurrences to individuals and small groups in the presence of God and then translating the experience wholesale into a staged mass event.

'Words of knowledge' are a case in point. In the Bible they occur within the context of personal relationships where they can be immediately confirmed or not. In a large audience setting they risk becoming a party piece in which only those which are confirmed find a home and the rest are mercifully forgotten. I have come to believe that the mass conference at which such things are stimulated is potentially corrupting. It becomes much harder to distinguish what might be a genuine response to the presence of God from the psychological and psychic pressures produced by a large group. This is not to say that good things do not happen but that there is a gravitational pull by the event setting itself in an unhelpful direction. For this context there is little justification in Scripture, but this itself is not the point; there are pressures set up which might stimulate phenomena unhelpfully.

There are also unpleasant temptations for those who lead such events to be seen to 'come up with the goods' by the audience in order to validate their own position and ministry. The expectation that unusual phenomena will happen and ought to happen conditions people in a way which cannot avoid the accusation of auto-suggestion or manipulation. I by no means reject the possibility of phenomena being part of a genuine response to God's presence but I am unashamedly persuaded that the best pastoral administration of them requires their being played down and not up. Sobriety and understatement are the best policy.

The person originally used to 'impart the Spirit' to John Wimber's church was called Lonnie Frisbee who had been previously active in the Jesus Movement. It was he whom John invited to minister when the team first came to Ansdell and through whom things 'happened'. I continue to be worried by a remark Lonnie passed in my hearing to the effect that even before he became a Christian he could make such things happen. Ever since I have wondered whether the 'wonders' that belong to the Vineyard tradition are as much psychic as they are spiritual. This might indicate that the supposedly supernatural events associated with John and the Vineyard are explicable on the human level by reference to those energies and forces which exist in the realm of the personal and group unconscious. Usually they are suppressed, but occasionally someone like Lonnie comes along with the capacity to unlock them. When this happens some trauma may be released, but generally it is a pleasurable experience to have hidden energies unlocked since this brings a sense of renewal and release with it. An under-discussed element in the Wimber (or now Toronto) phenomenon is that it can be great fun: the real question is, how Christian is it?

Many Christians, including John himself, operate with a highly dualistic worldview: things that happen are either of God or the devil. I don't accept this because it neglects the whole element of the 'natural', the realm of the created and of the merely human. Those therefore who deny that unusual phenomena are of God and so must be necessarily occultic are as mistaken as those who refer them uncritically to the action of God. It seems to me that they should be understood as aspects of our total religious experience as human beings. They could be human responses to the divine presence. Alternatively they could be merely human experiences which, because they happen in a particular context within a religious framework, are given a religious interpretation and even serve to further a religious purpose. In either case we would do well to be neither too condemnatory nor too impressed by them. They are things that happen within the diversity of religious experience. We should observe them and make sure that we channel them in the right directions without over-valuing them or seeing them as indicators of spirituality.

Thoughts like this must have occurred a thousand times to John and his associates, and it would be of great interest to me if he could at some point reflect upon them. The difficulty is that it is not easy to be critical of one's own practice without bringing a degree of hesitation to it. There is such a thing as the 'paralysis of analysis', as I have myself found in ministering in this area. Early in his ministry in this country I heard John speak in cautionary tones about the American drive to promote things. Ideas or products had no sooner been conceived than they are being marketed in the public forum. When you have a large-scale conference ministry to maintain in several continents it must be difficult to avoid this syndrome, especially when the troops are gathering waiting for the next instalment of wisdom, encouragement and guidance. It is easy to be impressed by what seems to work and this accounts in my perception for the wrong direction temporarily assumed when the 'Kansas City prophets' were incorporated into the team. Californian pragmatism which starts with what seems to be the administration of God's power, and then attempts to rationalise it theologically, is not always the best way to proceed. I am particularly grateful that in this instance John was able to steer the Vineyard ship around. But this said, any movement which assumes power and influence does need to subject itself to critical scrutiny and to invite that from others.

From the beginning John has declined to engage in self-justification before the bar of his critics. I understand the reason for this – not to respond to revilings with revilings – this is both typical and commendable. But there is also that duty which we all have to listen to what others may be saying to us about ourselves or our project, to make mid-course corrections in our journey and to indicate publicly that we have learnt from our critics. For the health of the Body of Christ we need this.

My final words must however be words of appreciation. A recent thorough study of Wimber's theology and practice by a thoughtful (and critical) commentator is built around the thesis that Wimber's 'power religion' puts God's love at the service of his power rather than his power at the service of his love. I might believe this criticism to be true of some who 'minister in power', even of some who minister in the Wimber network. But I do not finally believe it to be true of John Wimber himself. I recall times in 1982 when as a learner I stood alongside John as together we observed people being prayed for and ministered to. I was able to listen to his running commentary on what was happening for individuals and sense what was in his heart. It is one of his principles that when people are prayed for, even if the ministry does not deliver the healing they might desire, such ministry should be one of the most loving experiences they have ever had. There are things I envy about John Wimber: his relaxed, easy and laid-back approach, for instance, and his ability to communicate with thousands; but the thing I have most learnt from him and desire to practise is the priority of loving acceptance of others and of dealing with them with tenderness and love.

CHAPTER FIVE

Chris Woods

Chris Woods (b. 1943) is vicar of the parish of Holy Trinity, Parr Mount, in the diocese of Liverpool. After a business career in overseas marketing, he was ordained at the age of thirty-three and has been at Parr Mount since September 1979. Married to Kathy, a practising Roman Catholic, they have five children. Chris is a trustee of Anglican Renewal Ministries and Down to Earth Trust, and is on the Support and Advisory Group of Ellel Ministries.

The first time I met John Wimber was after a normal Sunday service at Anaheim in March 1988. My wife and I and our then four children were on our way back from a visit to New Zealand. We were staying with Vineyard friends in California, and we decided to attend church at Anaheim in the morning. My eldest daughter, Isabella, and I simply went up to John after the service, introduced ourselves and shook his hand, passing some small talk about how blessed we had been by his ministry during the past few years.

The second occasion I met him was in Manchester at the end of August 1993, just before the beginning of a Vineyard Conference at the Free Trade Hall. The senior pastor of the Manchester Vineyard, Martyn Smith, had asked me to open the Conference with an introduction and prayer from the platform. Later that day there was a brief team meeting with John, and I was introduced.

I owe much to John's teaching and ministry since first seeing and hearing him at St Andrew's, Chorleywood in October 1982. My wife, Kathy, and I had arrived in the parish of Holy Trinity, Parr Mount, St. Helens, in September 1979. It is one of the most deprived parishes in the Liverpool diocese; but we were full of enthusiasm and felt that we could 'turn it round' in a couple of years. We had already experienced a new filling with the Holy Spirit before arriving – myself during a Renewal Week at St Michael-le-Belfry in 1978, and Kathy about a year later. What we had not taken into account were the antagonistic attitudes of many members of the existing congregation. When I asked one prominent member of the church why several of my immediate predecessors as vicar had lasted only three or four years, his answer – without the glimmer of a smile – was, 'We saw them off' !

After our first few months in the parish, I realised that some urgent and persistent prayer was vital, and so I would get up at 6 am and try to spend about an hour with the Lord. I took these times very seriously, getting down on the floor, my face in the carpet, and wrestling with the Lord over the pastoral problems facing us. Looking back, I think that these times of prayer laid a spiritual foundation for some of the blessings that came later. But at the time, I experienced only immense frustrations and disappointments. One family of new Christians I was particularly praying for came under enormous pressures and the husband tried to kill himself. Another family of committed believers split up, despite my earnest intercession on their behalf. We had not at this time even heard the expression 'spiritual warfare' and therefore we were struggling from a position of great spiritual ignorance. Also, the traditional members of the congregation were intent on resisting every suggestion I made to try and reach out to the community where we lived. At one point I had a confrontation with one of the churchwardens, who had been inexcusably rude to a new family just feeling their way into the church. In a two-hour meeting in my study I said to him, 'You are spending all your time trying to keep people out of this church; I am spending twenty-four hours a day trying to get them in. There is no room for both of us, and I am not leaving!' Sadly he left, threatening to write to the Bishop.

The reason I am going into some detail about our early struggles is to highlight the differences which followed after our exposure to John Wimber's teaching and ministry. My wife and I believed we were 'Spirit-filled Christians', but somehow we didn't seem to have any effectiveness in reaching the neighbourhood where we lived. Yet, after we had seen and heard John, things were able to change.

After two years of these kinds of pressures I experienced the first major 'breaking' in myself when I was forced to confess to the Lord, 'I simply cannot cope with this.' And it was in this despairing and exhausted frame of mind that I attended an Anglican Renewal Ministries Conference at Swanwick in September 1981. On the way there I asked the Lord to let me meet someone who might be able to help us. At the very first meal I sat next to a man who turned out to be a member of St Andrew's, Chorleywood's Faith-Sharing team. This man told me that the leader of the team, Barry Kissell, was at the conference and that he would introduce me. When I met Barry I explained my situation and he suggested that he came with his team for a weekend mission to the congregation, to be followed up later by a longer mission to the parish. I readily agreed to this. But I was very disheartened when Barry said that the earliest date they could make would be 'November next year'! This seemed an eternity away to me.

About a month before the visit in November 1982, Barry rang us to ask if we could come down to Chorleywood to hear a man called John Wimber speak. Barry himself had already been powerfully influenced by this man's ministry, and he wanted us to have some experience of it before his visit, because he would attempt to minister among us in the style that John was modelling. It was very short notice, and Kathy and I could only manage to go down for the Friday, the first day of the Vineyard's full weekend visit to St Andrew's.

What we saw and heard that day had a profound effect on us. We had never before come upon such an openness in a person ministering in the power of the Spirit. We had seen one or two Pentecostal preachers in full swing, and the model had not been helpful. When I look back, I can't help smiling at my own inexperience in matters which have since become so normal in church life.

For example, at the end of the afternoon session, John simply invited the Holy Spirit to come upon us, and then walked among the congregation inviting us to look and 'see' the Spirit moving on a person. At the time I had no idea what to look for, or how to look at a person with any spiritual discernment at all. I remember a Baptist minister, who had been next to me all day, suddenly sitting down hard on the pew with a dazed look on his face and I stared at him wondering what was wrong. Meanwhile people were falling down or weeping quietly, not to mention the man who had stepped into the aisle before lunch and fallen on the floor, shouting and pounding the carpet with his fist. Wimber didn't move a muscle, remained standing behind the lectern and quietly said something like, 'I think this person is suffering from some deep hurts from childhood . . . '

All this was something out of another dimension for Kathy and me. We couldn't imagine such scenes happening in a David Watson meeting!

Short as our time had been at Chorleywood, God was speaking to us. As we drove back up the motorway to St Helens, I felt God say to me, 'What daily newspaper do you read?'

My answer was: *The Times*.

'What paper do the people around you read?'

'Well, the *Sun*, the *Daily Mirror* . . . '

'WHY do you read *The Times*?'

'Because I'm a person who likes to read discussions and articles of interest in a newspaper of about thirty-six pages of close print.'

'Why do the people among whom you are ministering read the tabloids?'

'Because they want to *see* what is going on, not read endless words about it.'

I felt God say, 'If you will let them *see me do something*, they will respond.' And then I saw vividly the truth of this principle: if local people *saw* God do powerful things, they would respond to his love in a way that they never could to words alone. This principle has held true to the present day (1 Cor 4:20).

So when Barry and his team arrived the following month, at least Kathy and I could cope with some of the things that happened even in that short weekend. Barry has described it in his book *Walking on Water*. We still had no theology for what we saw, but the style and honesty of the ministry were opening our minds to what was to come later.

By this time one or two local people were beginning to come to faith, through infant baptism requests, contacts at the local primary school, and so on, and in the summer of 1983 things began to move in more positive ways. This was as a direct result of the arrival in the church of the Rev Bob and Mary Hopkins (former members of Barry's Faith-Sharing team), Tim Humphrey, a young graduate friend of theirs from Chorleywood, and a full-time stipendiary curate, the Rev John Walker and his wife Michele. Our 'professional' team therefore suddenly expanded, just as we began a series of evangelistic events.

Barry Kissell came back in November 1983 for a ten-day mission in the parish. This took the form of evangelistic house-group meetings in the first week, followed by three days of preaching/teaching and ministry in the church building in the second week. The principles that Barry had assimilated from John Wimber's teaching were much to the fore. A number of people were brought to Christ and several experienced healings of various kinds. The power of the Holy Spirit was very evident. Some of those people who were powerfully touched during that mission are with us today.

This was in the days of Mission England and, as part of the local programme, we ran a 'Down-to-Earth' mission with Eric Delve for three full weeks in March 1984. This was followed in July by the visit of Billy Graham, who preached for a week at Anfield football ground in Liverpool. Over 100 people joined Holy Trinity through those months, almost every single one needing continuous help with domestic, social and personal problems. Our leadership team was swamped as we had no other mature Christians in the congregation who could help the newcomers. As a result, sadly, many fell through the net.

But this led us on to November 1984 with the first 'Signs and Wonders' Conference at Westminster Central Hall in London. We took about sixteen members, almost all new Christians, to London, somehow finding accommodation for everyone. It was this Conference above all which freed up Holy Trinity. Those who were there will never forget some of the extraordinary happenings. I remember attending a healing seminar led by Wimber's associate, Blaine Cook, at the end of which the Holy Spirit moved in great power. Again I found myself a spectator as amazing physical manifestations went on all around me. I used to travel widely round the world as a businessman before I was ordained, and I had seen many bizarre happenings and sights in various parts of Africa, the Middle East and India; but I felt God say to me in that seminar. 'You think you have seen a few things: just take a look at what is going on around you under the power of my Spirit!'

In the main meetings I noticed that the people we had taken down from St Helens couldn't wait for John Wimber to stop talking so that the ministry in the power of the Spirit could begin! One local man standing next to me said with absolute conviction, 'This is for us.' I agreed and found myself at last getting hold of the theological grid from which John was working. I may say that this has remained immensely helpful ever since. I have found his teaching on worldview enormously helpful and convincing from my own world travels. Also the kingdom of God teaching, with its inclusion of the spiritual warfare dimension, suddenly gave me the background for a theology which I have held on to ever since.

Over the next few months I found I was developing teaching gifts which had never previously been to the fore in my ministry, because I had never before had a coherent understanding of the way reality unfolds in the spiritual realm. Here was a credible biblical grid on which I could at last hang the things I was learning, and also the various elements of theology which I had picked up over the previous hectic years.

Again, John's integrity in demonstrating the Vineyard healing model from the platform was a revelation to me. There were clear explanations and histories recounted of people *not* being healed, but at the same time there was a 'demonstration of the Spirit's power', and testimonies from the Conference itself, which showed that healings were taking place under his ministry.

Another memorable seminar at the Westminster Conference was one for ordained men and women and pastors. Many hundreds of people were present, and I was deeply shocked when a large number manifested demons during the powerfully anointed ministry time. I can remember one dear man in a clerical collar on his hands and knees in front of the stage barking like a dog. As always, John didn't turn a hair. He encouraged us to examine our hearts and not to be distracted by what was going on around us.

We returned to St Helens very fired up to see what God was going to do among us. An immediate blessing was that a Vineyard team from the Westminster Conference was going to spend the next week at Ansdell Baptist Church, near Lytham St Anne's, less than an hour's drive from St Helens. We loaded up the church minibus every night with church members and sent it up to Lytham, and almost every person was powerfully touched by the Spirit at the meetings. We had bought tapes of the Westminster meetings, and with the help of the literature which was also provided, we began to teach through some of the 'signs and wonders' principles at our midweek Thursday night meetings in our church hall. We had freedom to do what we liked at these meetings, which was still not the case in Sunday worship, where I felt the constraints of the expectations of the older members.

These Thursday night meetings became the vehicle by which the Lord began to move powerfully by his Spirit in people's lives. We always made a time after any teaching to invite the Holy Spirit to come, and over a period of some years many signs and wonders were seen, including unbelievers coming to faith. We were being wonderfully led in worship throughout this time by Tim Humphrey, who was not only able to teach the principles of 'Presence worship', but also lead us into the practice of it. At about this time, I took the decision that we were going to worship in this way in Sunday services as well as on Thursday nights, and a number of the more traditional members reacted badly. But again, this was an area where John Wimber's teaching and ministry transformed our understanding and expectations of what was possible in the use of music.

Wimber's determination to 'equip the saints' and refuse to have dependency on the famous person on the platform was also a revelation to our local people. They found themselves praying for each other and their 'neighbour' with an effectiveness which no other model could have produced. Not only that, but I am certain that people coming from a very rudimentary educational background (as one of them admitted to me, 'most of us have never been to school, Chris') can have an openness to the moving of God's Spirit in circumstances which leave middle-class Christians refusing to enter in until they have had all their questions answered! Wimber's teaching on spiritual gifts therefore has added significance for us here.

After the Westminster Conference, we were so determined to see if what we had begun to learn actually worked in a church setting that six of us attended a Signs and Wonders course at Anaheim in February 1985. We stayed for two weeks in the area, billeted with different church members. We were fully convinced, not only by what we saw and heard again in the Conference, but also at home group meetings during the second week, that God was in all this. On the way back, I felt completely free to leave the Church of England, if that was what God wanted. At the same time I felt a confirmation of God's call to stay in it and see what transformations could happen from within.

In May of 1985 and again in 1986 we ran a Ministry in the Power of the Holy Spirit Conference in our church hall, attended by about 250 people from around Merseyside. Something happened on the first evening of the second conference which caused me to remain firmly committed to the style of inviting the Holy Spirit to come and for him to have his way.

I did that at the beginning of the ministry time on the Friday evening and a number of people were being touched by the Lord, with several people falling under the power of the Spirit. These included two people at opposite ends of the front row. Eventually they were taken through to a back room by members of our team, where a terrible story unfolded: the woman was the wife of an Anglican clergyman and the man was a married member of their church, and their avowed intention had been to go away together the following morning. But they had been unable to resist the sovereign power of the Holy Spirit and their plans came to nothing. As a result, two marriages were healed and restored. I am sure that this sort of story could be repeated time and again from local church sources such as ours. The reality is that if John Wimber had not introduced us to that style of ministry, I am certain nothing else we would have done would have exposed these sinful intentions in such an effective way.

Over the years since then we have had some hard struggles as a church. We have been both the fastest growing and then the fastest declining church in St Helens! For the past six years we have been in the process of developing a 'community-counselling' ministry. We are trying to reach into peoples' lives in a practical manner to help with some of the overwhelming problems that so many experience. One of the leaders of the oversight committee is one of our congregational lay leaders, a GP who runs a local surgery. We are very mindful of a recent BMA statistic which said that between 60% and 70% of people are visiting their GP for non-medical reasons.

Many members of the church have already been ministered to in the mixture of spiritual and practical ways which is so vital in this neighbourhood. Throughout the training of the team we have never found it necessary to depart from John's basic principles and models. We have had a lot of other input, particularly in the areas of inner-healing and deliverance, but our practising of spiritual discernment and actual prayer style continue to be fundamentally the Wimber five-step healing model.

The great breakthrough has been that, since our first exposure to John's teaching and practice, we have had a theology on which to work our ministry, and a style of operating which has been a blessing to many. Right from the start we have been open to seeing God move in power, either on a group or with individuals. We have not only been open, we have been expectant. We have been greatly helped also by other more detailed aspects of John Wimber's teaching, in particular: worship, spiritual warfare, spiritual gifts, kinship groups, church planting, and church planning. We have twice been through the workbook associated with the church planning teaching and have renewed our goals and priorities (what we spend time, energy and money on) accordingly. That teaching in itself has been liberating for me as pastor of the church – if only we were taught these simple but profoundly important matters in theological college!

We are now in our seventeenth year here – the social problems have become far worse over this period in terms of crime, violence, drug addiction, family breakdown and child abuse. (This local government ward has the highest breaking-and-entering statistics on Merseyside. We have had over twenty thefts and burglaries at the Vicarage alone.) I can truthfully say that given all the very marvellous teaching and ministry models we have been exposed to over the years, there is absolutely no doubt in my mind that we would have got nowhere without the things we have learnt from John Wimber and the Vineyard's ministry.

Even in the controversial area of prophecy we have been encouraged by the good things that came out of John Wimber's interest in the prophetic over the years, to develop a very accurate and dependable prophetic ministry, led by one especially gifted person. We have felt the freedom to do this because of the teaching, and the mistakes, of the Vineyard in the past few years.

As one meets so many discouraged people labouring in the Urban Priority Areas of this country, the advice the Church of England gives them is, 'Get a better insurance company'!

The advice we have had from John Wimber is, 'Get equipped, get empowered, and believe that God can and will do all that the Bible tells us he will.'

CHAPTER SIX

Gerald Coates

Gerald Coates (b. 1944) is leader of the Pioneer Team, that cares for around 100 churches across Europe and beyond, trains leaders and evangelists and works in partnership with other ministries to create fresh initiatives. Amongst these are the AIDS initiative ACET (AIDS Care Education Training) which he co-founded with Dr Patrick Dixon and of which he is now a Patron along with Sir Cliff Richard and Archbishop George Carey. With Ichthus/YWAM/Graham Kendrick he was one of the founders of the International March for Jesus. He has seven books to his credit, the last of which is The Vision – An Antidote to Post Charismatic Depression. *He is married to Anona and they have three grown-up sons. They live in Esher. Gerald also leads the church Pioneer People based in nearby Cobham, Surrey.*

It is said of some people, you either hate them or you love them.

John Wimber is such a man!

Most who have met him find him charming, gracious and attentive to a point of curiosity. No one can be this generous, surely? Perhaps such reactions are more a reflection of our own impatience and self interest. Many Christian leaders are under so much pressure they sound and act like Larry the Lamb on speed!

That is not to say that all of those who know John Wimber and love him agree with him. I have heard him make what I regard to be astounding statements regarding his understanding of Scripture eg, that there are no apostles today. Perhaps, having got burned by the Kansas City Prophets he has even questioned the nature of prophetic ministry! When it comes to the issues of women in leadership and ministry, there has been a resounding silence. Nevertheless, he is highly respected by Christian leaders who hold altogether different views regarding apostolic ministry, the prophetic and women in leadership and ministry. It is that generous heart and pleasant smile again.

John Wimber had been coming to the UK for many years prior to my first meeting with him at Westminster Central Hall in 1984. A friend of mine had met John in America at a conference. Having gained access to the man, and having been given a considerable amount of time, he was able to tell him what the Spirit of God was doing in the UK, and on this occasion, particularly through the New Church networks. John had a close relationship with David Watson and a large place in the heart of Anglican charismatic evangelicalism. He was largely unaware of what was the House Church Movement, commonly called New Churches by sociologists today.

'You must meet him,' my friend urged. But meeting and spending time with fairly well protected and relatively high-profile people like John Wimber was not quite as easy as my friend was suggesting.

Nevertheless, I wanted to hear the man speak, and find out what the growing controversy was all about. Having given up on driving from my home in Esher, Surrey, to Westminster – due to the fact it took more time to find a place to park than drive there – I took the train and then a taxi from Waterloo Station. I believe in coincidences, but this one was remarkable. As the taxi drove away from the front door of Westminster Central Hall, I turned and began the brief journey up the rather grand staircase into the building. Glancing to my right, ascending the steps with me, was John Wimber and his charming wife Carol! The astonishing thing was, having introduced myself somewhat briefly he appeared both to know all about me and our work in Pioneer. He was keen to talk. As we lunched he seemed genuinely interested in the New Churches and asked many questions about my colleagues Roger Forster and Terry Virgo, who up until that time were merely names he had come to respect.

It would be fair to say I have never been a disciple of John Wimber as such. Perhaps my broad range of interests and even broader network of relationships, and the fact that he lives in America and I in England, have contributed to that. And yet he is such an intriguing figure. A prolific author, his books are well researched and not merely laced with Scripture but in many cases exegeting and unpacking the Scriptures themselves. I say this because his style, laid back to the point of being laid down, can give an impression of shallow spontaneity. This belies the truth.

My second encounter with John Wimber was in his absence! John had previously conducted a large conference at a venue in the London area. Pioneer, the network of churches I am privileged to serve in a leadership capacity, had made a request to hire the venue for our own event some time later. My secretary was asked on the phone if there would be 'any healings'. Given the fact that the leaders of this denomination were evangelical it seemed rather odd. She was told that 'after John Wimber there would be no more healing'. I discussed this with one or two friends and eventually it got into the Christian press. I was then contacted by the leaders of this denomination and called to a meeting at the said venue. It was extremely frosty to put it politely!

John Wimber and a team from America had used rooms they had not hired, for counselling, prayer and deliverance.

One of the leaders of the venue told me he didn't 'believe in all this deliverance stuff' and clearly considered much within the charismatic movement as trivia and twaddle. He also began to sound like Larry the Lamb on speed. A plot was now emerging!

He explained further that after these people had left the chapel he had to 'exorcise it' with disinfectant. By now I was in a reactionary attitude. 'But I thought you didn't believe in demons,' I quipped, 'so what on earth were you exorcising from the chapel?' I thought he was going to hit me.

Months later this leader and I found ourselves on the same platform speaking at a conference. The issues were unresolved though we had been begrudgingly given the venue we had asked to hire. I realised it was no good waiting for him to apologise to me. No matter what he thought of John Wimber, exorcism and the use of their premises, my own attitude had been less than Christ-like. I later wrote and apologised and my letter was graciously acknowledged.

Generally speaking, American evangelical churches, including those of the Charismatic/Pentecostal variety, are considerably more legalistic than our British counterpart. Numerous British Christian leaders as long as twenty years ago began to hit out at the legalism involving quiet times, Sabbath keeping, the drinking of wine and beer and generally enjoying oneself. The difficulty was that many Christians, including Christian leaders, were not having quiet times but were having the occasional glass of wine, but they didn't let people know. I remember quipping on several occasions to now well-known personalities within the Christian world, 'If you are a secret drinker what else are you doing secretly?' The following story shows John Wimber has few secrets.

Whilst in London my wife Anona and I took John and Carol out to *Ménage à Trois* in Beauchamp Place in Knightsbridge.

'What would you like to drink?' I enquired, not knowing whether it would be Perrier or orange and ice.

'Do you know what I would really like?' he replied like a gleeful child. 'A large glass of Barsac.'

This was a wine I had been introduced to previously. It was sweet, full and quite difficult to get hold of, though not expensive. I ordered a bottle from the waitress as I was partial to a glass myself. It never arrived. The order for our food was taken and again we ordered the wine. Then having been there almost half an hour the wine waiter arrived to ask what we would like!

'This is the third time I have ordered this,' I said somewhat embarrassingly.

He apologised. 'This is a wine normally taken with puddings, Sir.'

John was now embarrassed. 'Give me a glass of water,' he shrugged with a nonchalant air of a man who wasn't fussed. But I was. Despite the absurdities of the notion that white wine goes with fish, red with meat and sweet wine with puddings he got his glass of Barsac!

So there it was again. The West Coast, laid-back generous, couldn't care less, we have got all the time in the world attitude. Or was this a grace of the Holy Spirit?

More seriously, it occurred again when one of his key leaders succumbed to sexual temptation. My somewhat hazy recollection is that I had expressed concern about this brother and the way he related to women – noticing the reaction of some of the women in my own church. Women are our radar!

But I seem to recall my perspectives were a mere mention. I certainly didn't think much of it. Alongside the fact that Vineyard are not known for their brilliant administration (a UK perspective!) I don't ever recall hearing from John about the matter. But shortly before Anthony Worral Thompson became chef of another restaurant we made a final visit to *Ménage à Trois*. As we walked down Beauchamp Place on that hot summer evening John put his arm around me and said, 'I really want to thank you for the generous way you dealt with the issues surrounding my friend caught in sexual immorality.'

He went on and on about my wisdom, clarity and the process by which we dealt with such matters. I confess I had not a clue what he was talking about. I wondered if he was confusing me with somebody else with another incident. He told close friends of mine Sandy Millar and Terry Virgo, 'If only I had the grace to deal with things the way Gerald did.'

To this day I often wonder whether he mixed me up with Father Christmas, Batman or Mother Teresa!

Either way, it is the generosity of spirit that has left its mark on my own ministry. One final illustration to underline this important perspective of the Wimber phenomena.

'London for Jesus – Together We Stand' consists of various streams and groupings that work in and around London, working together. Roger Forster of Ichthus, Sandy Millar of Holy Trinity, Brompton, Colin Dye of Kensington Temple and Lynn Green of Youth With A Mission Europe and myself have been privileged to gather up to 11,000 believers to pray for revival in the land.

On one occasion at the suggestion of Sandy Millar, we took London's Royal Albert Hall which seats over 5,500 people. John Wimber was passing through and was invited to speak at the meeting. For those who know it, the Royal Albert Hall can be a wonderful experience as it affords a high feel-good factor, intimacy and therefore great atmosphere. Worship was already under way when Sandy and Annette Millar brought John onto the stage to join in the worship. Sandy Millar is an artist in the skill of understatement. I don't think John Wimber had the first clue what he was coming to. He was taken through rear doors and corridors, up back steps onto the stage, and sat for a short while to gain his equilibrium. He prayed. Looking up he suddenly saw

5,500 people, in boxes on the balcony, in the stalls and in the arena and he just broke down and wept. In fact he wept right the way throughout the whole meeting.

He told me some months later when he was back in England that he couldn't believe that we had done this for him. Given the fact that his church is moving toward the size of the congregation at the Royal Albert Hall, I was bemused by the comment. Yet again he showed a generosity of spirit and an appreciation for the work that had been put into filling the Royal Albert Hall for his ministry.

As it happened he was no sooner under way than he had a word of knowledge for a lady with a disability. He prayed for her and as I recall she collapsed on the floor though she was never asked forward. Visiting Sandy and Annette's home two or three weeks later, I heard that this lady who moved with great difficulty was now 'running around Hyde Park, wonderfully healed'.

Invariably our strength becomes our weakness. The down side of John Wimber's generosity and openness to other ministries and his desire to learn from others is that he has tended to live his life in a goldfish bowl. By that I mean that every relationship, every friendship and every new emphasis in his own ministry is in the glare of at least the Christian media if not others within a very short while. Short-term relationships that have never been tested are exposed (to my mind) prematurely. They often collapse later on. It is therefore not surprising that a number of relationships John has enjoyed and ministries he has stood alongside have ended in tension within a fairly short time. Due to that same generosity of spirit, many have found a high degree of reconciliation some time later. But I have often wondered whether or not it would have been better for some of these relationships to be nurtured in private and strengthened through fellowship, prayer, eating and drinking before they went so public.

One still hears of 'John Wimber and the Kansas City Prophets', or 'John Wimber and Paul Cain', as though they live in each other's pockets to this day. This, they do not. But we are left with this and other impressions through the media even though they are false at times. And a perception can be as important as reality. But for all of that, as the old adage points out, it is better to have tried and failed than not to have tried at all. The British are conservative and cautious and need to be shaken up by our American friends and their entrepreneurial spirit. Whilst the American church is awash with naiveté, the British church is awash with cynicism. It does not have to be either/or but it seems like that sometimes. So while the cynics scoff that the healer cannot heal himself, John Wimber carries on, sometimes even in a wheelchair.

History is full of those with disabilities both intellectual and physical, emotional and even spiritual, whom God used in extraordinary ways. Why does he do it? If only God would use the sort of people we think he should use! But healthy or sick, standing or sitting, John is a man who has endeavoured to fulfil his commitments, serve the church, whether he is emotionally up or down, in favour or under criticism. In answer to why he is not healed, he is open and genuine enough to simply say, 'I don't know.' That is maturity. We are often looking for answers whereas God is looking to give us his discernment and wisdom irrespective of whether we have any answers.

In the late 1960s and early 1970s a few young men in their mid-twenties were baptised in the Holy Spirit. They did not come from Anglican churches and therefore did not go through the normal training procedure in the hope of becoming a vicar or rector, bishop or ultimately an archbishop! These came from primarily Baptist or Brethren churches. With a heritage of a measure of separation and independency it was more easy for these (than those in other denominations) to meet in homes with friends to pray. With the new dynamic of the gifts of the Spirit, following their baptism in the Holy Spirit, these small fairly private inoffensive groups became very attractive. Within a few years, many of these men found themselves with dozens, or even scores of people wanting to identify with them. Whilst they still met in homes, they also met in cinemas and school halls to accommodate the slow but nevertheless growing numbers.

Around twenty-five years later, of the one-and-a-quarter million evangelicals in Britain, around 60% are charismatic/ pentecostal. Even more astonishing is that the number of people in what the sociologists now call New Churches (formerly house churches as against traditional denomination churches) is almost a quarter of a million! Around half of these are in networks led by people like Terry Virgo, Bryn Jones, Roger Forster and myself.

As already mentioned, John Wimber had heard of some of the leaders of this movement in the early 1980s, but had never met them. It was perhaps difficult for him to understand the phenomena of New Churches, as America is littered with church breaks, splits, independency and the such. He would not be unaware of the fact that there are around 22,000 denominations of the world. However, when I was a boy, you were either Catholic or Anglican, Baptist or Methodist, Salvation Army or Brethren, Elim or Assembly of God. We didn't know there were any more denominations than that!

But despite John's own ecclesiology, and his strong links to the Anglican church through David Watson, he instinctively knew there was life, flexibility and growth within these New Churches and it wasn't long before he found himself meeting a number of New Church leaders. Not only that, but he was happy to respond to invitations to private meetings, occasional leaders' meetings, and indeed, gave Terry Virgo in particular, a number of platforms at his Vineyard conferences, both in the UK and overseas. Singer/songwriter, Noel Richards, has been to Anaheim for major events and has also taken part in a number of Vineyard-related conferences and celebrations.

But what effect has John Wimber had on the New

Churches? After all, they were already exercising the gifts of the Spirit, and were not bound with the legalism of parts of classic Pentecostalism.

What Wimber brought into them was something more than simply speaking in tongues and interpreting them, prophesying and quietly (and almost always privately) praying for the sick. He 'invited' the Holy Spirit to come into meetings which went beyond simply exercising the gifts of the Spirit. Some of the laughter, tears and certainly the jerking associated with the 'Toronto blessing' was, in fact, seen under John Wimber's ministry almost fifteen years ago. But it was unorchestrated. There were no catchers or tapes on the floor to administrate large numbers, and it was a miracle that people weren't hurt as they collapsed into piles of chairs or on to other people.

What John Wimber brought to the New Churches, then, was a much broader expression and experience of the work of the Spirit. Wimber's approach gave them a sense of the imminent presence of God, simply to bless and encourage them at his nearness. Into that setting came deliverance, either from demons or strongholds; and whilst spiritual warfare has always been a controversial issue, John Wimber would probably subscribe to my notion that at the most basic level, a stronghold is whatever has a strong hold on a person or a people.

The other and important aspect of Wimber's impact upon the New Churches was Power Evangelism. Throughout the 1970s, most of those who were a part of the growing movement were either disillusioned or disaffected evangelicals in denominational churches. I have no doubt many would never have continued in those churches, some of whom were led by non-evangelicals and a few anti-evangelicals. They would have been lost to God and to the church. So having new avenues within these New Churches has done the church at large an enormous amount of good. However, there were only a few that were coming to Christ from an unchurched background, and their success at reaching the lost and seeing the unchurched come to Christ was no greater or lesser than many of the churches they had come from. From those early days, with limited fruit to show for their evangelism, New Church leaders and many of those following them have always had a vision to see their relational or geographic area impacted with the gospel.

So when John Wimber came along with Power Evangelism, in giving the lost or those on a journey to faith an experience of the Spirit, the New Churches were ready for the message. There was a far greater boldness to pray with the unchurched, to expect 'something to happen', whether in the realm of healing, or a 'Power Encounter'.

It is interesting to note that almost every New Church network has also been deeply impacted by Toronto, which was simply seen as another wave of the Holy Spirit, not dissimilar to what had come out of Wimber/Anaheim. It may have been administrated a little differently, particularly in Toronto, under John Arnott's leadership, primarily because of the colossal numbers packing into their original building and greater numbers into their present one. New Church leaders I meet with on a regular basis, all see a mixture of manifestations of the Spirit, or reactions to the Spirit's presence, that one saw under Wimber's ministry in the 1980s as well as under Arnott's in the 1990s.

After the colossal growth of the New Churches, twenty-five years after they began, they have had to ask important questions of themselves, about themselves. On the one hand it's a colossal success story with over 2,000 churches in their networks and national and in some cases, international, ministries coming out of New Church relationships such as the AIDS initiative, ACET, the prayer initiative, March for Jesus, the teaching magazine, *Compass*, the largest Bible week, Stoneleigh, and literally hundreds of other local, national and international initiatives. But on the inside, the feel is quite different. These leaders have looked for so much and at one level, it's come to so little. Crime, in general, is on the increase, poverty is on the increase, there's been a break-up of the monarchy in the last twenty-five years. Either purposefully, or naively, they thought the New Churches would be the answer to the apostasy and apathy of the church at large. So the last twenty-five years has been the best of times and in another respect, the worst of times.

Just as John Wimber came along in the 1980s and, intentionally or otherwise, sowed Power Evangelism into a prepared field, so one of his churches which he later disengaged from, has brought a fresh wave of the Spirit – and this at the time when, after several years of plateauing, they are now geared for more evangelism, social action initiatives and church planting. Evangelisation and evangelism are high on most New Church agendas. There is also a new sense of expectancy and optimism among the apostolic team leaders, which is visibly and passionately expressed at leaders' events and Bible weeks. John Wimber and, it has to be said, John Arnott, are directly and indirectly one of the main causes, humanly speaking, of this new evangelistic thrust.

Despite Ele Mumford being the first to bring this special 'Toronto blessing' back from Toronto to England, her husband, John Mumford and most, if not all Vineyard churches in the UK, have remained loyal to John Wimber, despite the separation of Anaheim from Toronto. The leaders of these churches, whilst grateful to John Arnott in Toronto, are fully aware that if it were not for John Wimber they would not even be in existence. That is not the case in Ontario, other parts of Canada, and the USA. For while people have been deeply grateful and remain profoundly appreciative of John Wimber and his ministry, the blessing of the Spirit and the relationships that have come out of Toronto forced them to separate themselves from the Vineyard. They will probably end up in a new loose network where they would see John Arnott as a father figure.

It is true of any growing network of churches, just as it is in business, that the original founder and father figure can get more isolated and separated from those he started off with. So in the eyes of anyone from Toronto, it is fascinating to observe the loyalty and commitment to John Wimber from the UK churches. I am sure all leaders have their own perspective on the Wimber/Arnott relationship, the work of the Spirit and phenomena attached to their work, and other issues surrounding Anaheim and Toronto. But we should be grateful that God sees our hearts and minds, our successes and our failures, and sees things as they really are, not merely as we mortals see them.

There is no doubt that the hand of God has been on John Wimber and remains on him, despite continual public criticism of his ministry and theology, premature bereavement of some around him, and his own personal state of health. Only God knows the sacrifices he's made amid successes and failures, getting things right and getting things wrong. God himself will crown each of us, including John Wimber, for where we got it right, where we pioneered, and where we've displayed both the fruit and the gifts of God's spirit. It will then be that we see the real impact John Wimber has made not only on the New Churches but on the church at large, both in Europe and the Americas.

John Wimber has been closely associated with 'phenomena'. But Wimber is a remarkable phenomenon himself!

CHAPTER SEVEN

Mark Stibbe

Dr Mark Stibbe (b. 1960) is vicar of St Mark's Grenoside in Sheffield and an honorary lecturer in the Department of Biblical Studies at Sheffield University. Formerly he was curate at St Thomas' Church Crookes. He is the author of many books, including John's Gospel *(Routledge, 1995),* Times of Refreshing *(Harper Collins, 1995) and* O Brave New Church *(Darton Longman & Todd, 1995). His main interests have to do with the development of renewal theology.*

One of the turning points in my Christian life occurred at the 'Signs and Wonders' Conference in Sheffield (1985). At that time I had been a Christian for about ten years but had no real appreciation of the dynamic, supernatural dimension to the Christian faith. Up until then, most of my time had been spent with conservative evangelical friends who understood baptism in the Holy Spirit in terms of saying the sinner's prayer (as opposed to the climactic and experiential moment of Kingdom initiation), and who believed that the gifts of the Spirit had ceased at the end of the apostolic era. What turned my life upside-down at John Wimber's conference was a combination of his intelligent, biblical teaching on signs and wonders and the unmistakable evidence of 'God's empowering presence' in our midst. This caused a profound paradigm shift in my whole way of thinking. From then on, I saw that the Word and the Spirit, that doctrine and experience, must go together in our theology and praxis. Scripture and the power of God must not be ignored nor must they be separated (Matthew 22:29).

I therefore owe a great deal to John Wimber. The last day of the 'Signs and Wonders' Conference in Sheffield was a particularly significant moment for me personally. John was reading out the list of the fivefold ministries of the Spirit in Ephesians 4 when he came to the word 'teacher'. As he prayed for God to raise up and equip teachers my right hand started to shake. This was not something that had ever happened to me before. I therefore prayed that God would tell me what this experience *meant*. As I did so, an impression seemed to surface in my mind, 'I am anointing you to be a teacher in my church, and I am anointing your right hand so that you can teach by writing as well as by speaking.' At the time, although I had no ministry of speaking or writing (that was to begin seven years later), I sensed an inner excitement about this – a deep resonance that this was God, that this was right, and that this made sense. Ten years on, and eight books later, this impression has not left me!

With that in mind, I feel that there is a certain propriety in writing a chapter in this book. My particular contribution concerns the recent theological critique of Wimber's beliefs and practices. Wimber has come in for a good deal of criticism in the last few years. Not long ago I was surfing through Compuserve and the Internet and I was disturbed to discover how many trenchant criticisms there were directed against John Wimber, his ministry, and his congregations. Wimber is obviously not infallible in either his theology or his methodology. He is humble enough to admit that himself. Yet so much of what has been said about him lacks intellectual rigour that I feel bound to put the record straight. With that in mind I would like to look at the most recent and the most extensive theological critique of Wimber, Martin Percy's *Words, Wonders and Power* (London: SPCK, 1996). Though much of this book contains perceptive insights, some of it also contains weaknesses which typify the current attitude amongst Wimber's critics. My aim in this chapter will be to highlight these in order to pave the way for a fairer, more judicious assessment of Wimber's theology and ministry.

Martin Percy's book is subtitled, 'Understanding Contemporary Christian Fundamentalism and Revivalism'. It is important to mention this because his main purpose is to write about fundamentalism, using John Wimber as his *primum exemplum*. 'Once upon a time,' Percy writes, 'Christian fundamentalism was a religion for the few. Believers gathered together in tiny chapels, cut off from the storms of life and the reality of the world.' Now, however, things are very different. Today, fundamentalism is a worldwide force. Thirteen million viewers tune into fundamentalist TV stations every week. Fundamentalists influence elections, they scrutinise school curricula and they picket abortion clinics. As a result, fundamentalism must be taken seriously and it must be studied properly. What Percy seeks to provide in his book is an 'empathetic, critical and systematic analysis' of a movement which is 'alive and kicking in the post-modern world' (p 6). His aim is to describe those factors which bind the fundamentalist family together. According to Percy, *Words, Wonders and Power* is the first sustained attempt to analyse the 'power' of fundamentalism in a comprehensive way.

Percy starts with what he regards as the five characteristics of fundamentalism:

1. Fundamentalism legitimates present practices and beliefs by looking back to the past, especially to Scripture. In other words, fundamentalists justify what they believe and do by tracing a single line of development from the pages of an inerrant Bible to the present situation of the church.

2. Fundamentalism exists in relation to and in opposition to trends in society which it perceives as modernist. Fundamentalists therefore tend to engage in a holy war against liberalism, pluralism, and other 'isms' which are seen as hostile to the purity of its doctrinal position.

3. Fundamentalism represents a habit of mind rather than a movement. This 'habit of mind' is characterised by an attitude of enmity towards the world, and a corresponding set of fundamental beliefs with which to combat it.

4. Fundamentalism is a phenomenon which crosses all denominational boundaries and it is usually found where people rail against theological and ethical liberalism.

5. Fundamentalism is more than a system of beliefs; it is a cultural-linguistic system which employs 'myths' and narratives in order to structure human experience.

After thirteen pages about Christian fundamentalism in general, Percy suddenly tells us that the rest of his book is going to be a critique of John Wimber. Percy sees Wimber as a 'pre-eminent contemporary fundamentalist in the "revivalist tradition" ' (p 13). He attempts to justify this claim by showing how Wimber exhibits all five of the characteristics of fundamentalism just outlined. He contends that Wimber looks to the past to legitimise his present practice, and that he does this by affirming the doctrine of scriptural inerrancy! He claims that Wimber's theology stands in opposition to the trends of modernism and that it has established a set of fundamentals with which to combat it. Indeed, Percy argues that Wimber has been waging a holy war against the weak, powerless, dead churches of the world by using the 'highly mythical language of demons, powers and principalities' (p 14). He goes on to say that Wimber is trans-denominational in his influence, antagonistic towards other belief systems, and closed to the possibility of dialogue. In this respect, Percy regards Wimber as an excellent case-study. Wimber is a fundamentalist – albeit a 'sophisticated fundamentalist' (p 14).

Percy goes further. He provides a chapter on power, agency and charisma in which he argues that the understanding and use of 'power' in the Vineyard churches places Wimber firmly within the fundamentalist paradigm. According to Percy, the power evidenced in Wimber's churches is not a thing that exists independently. It is something which arises out of a 'circuit' involving the charismatic leader and his followers. This circuit is charged up by three factors common to fundamentalism: first, a charismatic message which offers a simplistic view of the world and an alternative to the *status quo* in a time of cultural stress; secondly, a charismatic personality who has high status, a tight control over people, an insistence on his 'ordinariness', a sense of a special vocation, sexual mystique, and the ability to behave in a dramatic way: and thirdly, 'delivery elements' – ie, the ability to communicate his message with eloquence and spellbinding power. In Percy's opinion, Wimber demonstrates all three of these; he has a charismatic message, personality and delivery. Since these three are stable features of fundamentalism, Percy reasons that John Wimber must be a fundamentalist.

Percy's argument, however, is flawed. His description of fundamentalism is so brief and abstract that almost any expression of Christianity could be used as an example – as Percy himself has the honesty to acknowledge (p 13). As a result, when we get down to the details, the differences between Wimber and 'fundamentalism' become as noticeable as the similarities. I happen to agree that there are some fundamentalist features in Wimber's theology, not least his hostility towards the Enlightenment (something about which Percy is oddly silent). However, Wimber also exhibits features which are not true of fundamentalists, even 'sophisticated fundamentalists' (an extraordinary oxymoron, surely). For example, Wimber does not possess 'sexual mystique', and Percy's attempt to claim otherwise by resorting to Wimber's 'aura of cuddliness' is unconvincing (p 59). Wimber is not a sex symbol, nor is he eloquent, dramatic, and sartorially refined. He is not tall, athletic, physically attractive, well-dressed, sensationalist and rhetorically gifted (like many truly fundamentalist preachers). In many ways, Wimber represents a resistance to fundamentalism rather than a refinement of it. The very core of Percy's thesis therefore seems rather unstable – a fact which becomes even more apparent when we look at Percy's analysis of the fundamental belief in Wimber's theology.

The core doctrine which Percy sees in Wimber's writings and teaching concerns 'power'. Most fundamentalists see power as something that lies in the texts of Scripture. For them, the power of God exists in the inerrant Word – hence the emphasis upon Bible exposition. For Wimber, however, the power of God is a invisible, intangible and supernatural phenomenon and it is located in the transrational work of the Spirit. Wimber sees power not only in the infallible Word of God, but also in the manifest activity of the Holy Spirit. This is the core doctrine, the basic belief, which undergirds his ideology and which fuels the fire of his polemic against modernism. The rest of *Words, Wonders and Power* is therefore taken up with a critique of Wimber's theology of power. Percy argues that this theology is open to serious criticism for the following reasons: because Wimber uses power for self-assertion; because human power (the charisma of the leader) is often conflated with divine power; because 'power' language results in a defensive attitude towards others; because there has been an attempt to own divine power rather than be owned by it; because an emphasis on power has created a mechanistic view of God's relationship with the world. In this respect, Percy argues that Wimber's core doctrine of power is dangerously suspect.[1]

I grant the fact that 'the power of God' is a recurrent, consistent theme in Wimber's teaching and life. That much is obvious to anyone; for evidence, you need look no further than the titles of two of his best-selling books, *Power Evan-*

gelism (London: Hodder 1985) and *Power Healing* (London: Hodder 1987). Once again, however, things are not as simple as Percy makes out. The core doctrine in Wimber's teaching is not 'the power of God' (or any other kind of power, for that matter). It is the 'kingdom of God' in the ministry and theology of the historical Jesus.[2] To be sure, power comes into that because Jesus taught with *exousia* (authority) and he performed mighty works (works of *dunamis* or power), and these are central characteristics of the kingdom. But to say that God's power is Wimber's core doctrine is inaccurate. The truth of the matter is this: John Wimber has, through intense study of the Bible and of scholarly, secondary literature (particularly the works of George Eldon Ladd), arrived at the conclusion that the kingdom of God is central in the teaching of Jesus, and that this kingdom is primarily manifested in authoritative proclamation with demonstrations of the Spirit's power. From here Wimber goes on to add that the church needs to recapture a sense of the rich, experiential reality of the kingdom if it is to be truly reflective of Jesus' teaching and truly effective in the post-modern world. The emphasis, in other words, is on the kingdom of God rather than the power of God.

Now I happen to believe – like Percy – that the appearance of 'power' in Vineyard meetings is caused by factors that can be explained psychologically and sociologically as well as spiritually. Percy's use of the social sciences is a valuable contribution towards a more holistic and rigorous understanding of this matrix of factors. But I disagree with Percy when he implies that these evidences of power are purely the product of social interaction. The most prominent weakness of this book is its failure to interact with the impressive testimony to the power of God in the pages of both the New Testament and in church history. Jimmy Dunn's book, *Jesus and the Spirit*, is an invaluable resource for examining the eschatological power of the Spirit in the life of Jesus and the early church.[3] Gordon Fee's analysis of the Spirit in the letters of Paul in *God's Empowering Presence* is another.[4] Neither, however, is mentioned in Percy's book. Even if Percy had been right to say that 'power' represents the core doctrine in Wimber's theology, I would have responded with the claim that this itself is a perfectly reasonable biblical viewpoint. In many ways, what Gordon Fee has recently said about the letters of Saint Paul sums up John Wimber's position perfectly:

> For Paul the Spirit, as an experienced and living reality, was the absolutely crucial matter for Christian life, from beginning to end. That, at least, is the contention of this book. For the contemporary church it seems much less so, both in the academy, in its understanding of Pauline theology, and in the actual life of the church . . . [5]

The weaknesses in Percy's research become even more evident in Chapter Four of his book, where we move on to the subject of Wimber's ideology, as seen in his worship songs. Percy argues that these songs reinforce Wimber's ideology in a monotonous and emotive manner.[6] They consistently emphasise the power of God to the detriment of other aspects of God's being and acts. Vineyard songs, Percy claims, neglect the following subjects: sin, the Cross, holiness, weakness, social justice and sharing in Christ's sufferings.[7] They reinforce submission to the power of God and also to 'the powers that be' through a constant use of the word 'Lord'. This attitude of 'passivity' before God and the hierarchy of the church is further strengthened through imagery of surrender. What matters is for the Christian believer to be in a passive, receiving mode before God and his anointed leaders. As Percy puts it, 'In metaphor, theme and form, a clear stress on submission to power emerges' (p 66).

After reading this chapter on worship I went straight to the volume, *Let Your Glory Fall*, a collection of 100 worship songs and essays expressing the core values behind the Vineyard's theology and practice of worship. I first of all checked the references to 'power' in the volume. Out of the 100 songs, only eight mentioned the noun 'power' or the verb 'empower'. That represents 8% of the total volume, hardly the overwhelming imbalance which Percy contends is a feature of Vineyard hymnody. Furthermore, in these eight songs, power is never the dominant theme; it is one theme amongst many. For example, in Kevin Prosch's very popular song, *Show Your Power* (Mercy Publishing, 1991), we have the following lines:

Your gospel O Lord, is the hope for our nation,
You are the Lord
It's the power of God for our salvation
You are the Lord
We ask not for riches, but look to the cross
You are the Lord
And for our inheritance give us the lost
You are the Lord.

Here, 'power' is not the 'brute supernatural force' claimed by Percy, nor is it a power reinforcing submission. This is 'the power of God for our salvation', a phrase taken directly from Romans 1.16 (a fact which tells against Percy's comment that the diction of Vineyard songs is not 'substantially biblical', p 68). Furthermore, 'power' is not the central, pivotal *topos* of the stanza; that privilege is reserved for 'evangelism' (reaching a lost nation for Christ). This emphasis on mission is important as well; it militates against Percy's claim that Vineyard songs are always self-orientated. Many Vineyard songs contain a passionate intercession for mission to the unchurched world.

Perhaps the most serious criticism which Percy makes of the songs of the Vineyard is that they focus on the power of the Spirit rather than the Cross of Christ. We have already seen from the statistical overview of *Let Your Glory Fall* that the first part of this claim (an overemphasis upon power) is wrong. The song, *Show Your Power*, also suggests that the second part (a neglect of the Cross) is wrong as well. Prosch writes,

> We ask not for riches, but look to the Cross.

Here, in direct contrast to what Percy says, the Cross is elevated as the *focus* of our devotion. The Cross and the Spirit (contra Percy) are united not divorced. Furthermore, this song is not the exception. A large number make the Cross and the Atonement a pivotal moment in their lyricism. Here are just a few examples:

> Gentle Lamb, fill me with kindness,
> Loving One, shine through my life,
> Brokenness flows through your nailprints,
> I am Yours, and you are mine
>
>   (Scott Brenner, 1995, Mercy/Vineyard).

> Jesus, You're everything that I've ever wanted,
> The blood you shed at Calvary has made me clean,
> You've drawn me back to You,
> And I would give you everything to be Yours forever,
> The sacrifice of love You shared has set me free
> To sail away with you
>
>   (Scott Brenner, 1995, Mercy/Vineyard).

> I know a place, a wonderful place
> Where accused and condemned
> Find mercy and grace
> Where the wrongs we have done
> And the wrongs done to us
> Were nailed there with him
> There on the Cross
>
>   (Randy & Terry Butler, 1993, Mercy).

> I am so thankful for the fullness of your love
> I am so thankful for the shedding of your blood

I am so thankful you died in my place
Oh Lord, I'm thankful for your love

   (Loren Bieg, 1994, Mercy/Vineyard).

Only the blood of Jesus
Covers all my sin
Only the life of Jesus
Renews me from within

   (Brian Doerksen, 1990, Mercy).

You are the worthy one
Lamb that was slain
You bought us with Your blood
And with You we'll reign

   (Andy Park, 1988, Mercy).

These examples show the very serious flaw in Percy's claim that the Cross is absent in Vineyard hymnody. It is very much a feature of the worship songs and indeed of the overall Vineyard theology of worship. As Scott Brenner writes,

> It is the fragrance of Christ Himself which makes our worship acceptable to God. Paul tells us in Ephesians that Christ loved us and therefore *gave himself up for us as a fragrant offering and sacrifice to God* (*Ephesians 5.2*). The sweetest fragrance of all to God is the fragrance of Christ's sacrifice for Himself on the cross for our benefit.[8]

If Percy's claim that the Cross 'is almost absent' (p 64) is misguided, so is his claim concerning the absence of other themes. Percy mentions sin as 'almost entirely absent' (notice the guarded use of the word 'almost' again). In the volume, *Let Your Glory Fall*, this is simply not the case. One of the most popular Vineyard songs of the 1990s so far is Brian Doerksen's *Refiner's Fire*, a song whose central petition is for holiness:

Purify my heart
Cleanse me from within and make me holy
Purify my heart
Cleanse me from my sin, deep within.

(1990, Mercy).

This is a noticeable theme in other songs by Doerksen, such as *Only the Blood* (1990, Mercy). Percy also argues that theme of 'power in weakness' is absent. Not so, as the following extracts testify:

You have chosen the weak things of the world
To shame that which is strong

(Kevin Prosch, 1991, Mercy).

It's our confession, Lord, that we are weak
So very weak,
But you are strong

(David Ruis, 1995, Mercy/Vineyard).

Percy also proposes that Wimber's songs never mention 'sharing in Christ's sufferings'. What about Bob Baker's song, *I Love You Forever*?

Oh may my life burn as an offering
That is pleasing unto thee
I'll count it joy to share your suffering
That your life may flow from me

(1994, Mercy/Vineyard).

Percy finally contends that the subject of 'solidarity with victims of human hurt' is 'completely absent' (p 81 – notice the change from 'almost' to 'completely'). Again, this is a debatable point. Even given the difficulty of making a topic like poverty the subject of a devotional song, we still have examples like *Spirit of the Sovereign Lord* by Andy Park (1994, Mercy).

In the final analysis, Percy's survey of Vineyard worship music is far too selective. It is simply wrong to say that these songs betray a *mutation* of God's nature – that is, a distorted picture of God. The key feature of Vineyard worship music is the notion of intimacy with a God of love. John and Carol Wimber understand worship as a lifestyle not just as singing songs, and this lifestyle involves 'the act of freely giving love to God'.[9] This lifestyle of self-giving to God is emphatically 'holistic' in the Vineyard movement. It is not just a matter of affirming doctrinal truths with the mind (what Percy seems to want it to be). It is an expression of a love for God which involves minds, hearts, hands, feet . . . everything! In this experiential, passionate worship, the Cross is regarded as central. As Carl Tuttle has put it,

> When we come to God, we come by the way Jesus bought for us through his blood. We come to God with confidence, and guiltless because of what Jesus did for us.[10]

In the final analysis, though there are weaknesses in some Vineyard songs, there is a significant corpus which has immeasurably enriched churches of all denominations, and which has also, I feel bound to say, enriched my own life. Percy's attempt to use Vineyard worship to prove his thesis concerning 'power' is simply not convincing.

Percy's thesis is that 'For Wimber, the heart of the Christian faith resides in an experience of the power and love of God, not in a creed' (p 33). This is suggested by Wimber's theology, which constantly stresses the omnipotence of God, by his Christology, which portrays Jesus as the supreme model of divine power, and by his pneumatology, which depicts the Holy Spirit as a dominant, all-conquering force. Percy says that inevitable problems arise from this militaristic faith. Wimber's soteriology portrays the Cross in terms of victory rather than suffering. As a result, weakness and suffering are given undue attention and everything is seen in terms of a stark dualism (Jesus versus Satan). As we have

seen, Percy uses the worship songs of the Vineyard in order
to prove his case; and elsewhere he tries to use Wimber's
ecclesiology (his understanding and organisation of the
church) as evidence too. Percy concludes that Wimber is a
symptom of the present social climate in which power and
experience are greatly esteemed. His movement has pros-
pered because of the widespread need for certainty in times
of traumatic, cultural instability. Wimber, in short, is a
sophisticated fundamentalist who has produced a sectarian
movement in which the power of love has been exchanged
for the love of power.[11]

Much of this will seem very odd to the many people who
know, love, and respect John Wimber. Indeed, many will
want to respond by saying that Percy has painted a portrait of
Wimber which is the furthest remove from the real person.
Percy's book appears to be a rational, scientific study but is,
in reality, inaccurate at a number of points and, worse still,
quite subjective. He seems to have a prior commitment to a
prejudicial view of Wimber, and this surfaces in emotive
adjectives like 'vacuous' which suddenly crop up in passages
of otherwise academic prose. It is revealed in the extraordinary charge of sectarianism (which is even described as 'tri-
bal' on p 135) – a charge which is hardly visible in Wimber's
commitment to dialogue with other denominations, including
the historic churches (particularly the Anglican and Roman
Catholic churches).[12] It is above all revealed in Percy's
insistence that 'power' forms the principle of coherence
throughout Wimber's teaching. As I have already argued,
Wimber's core doctrine concerns 'the kingdom of God',
not power. By putting 'power' at the centre of his critique,
and by using quite 'powerful' language in order to expose it,
Percy runs the risk of being hoisted by his own petard. In
other words, he runs the risk of being accused of using
'power' to combat 'power' (the very thing he is seeking to
condemn).

For me, the most regrettable aspect of Percy's book is the

way it treats John Wimber's kingdom theology as a static rather than an evolving phenomenon. The constant implication of the book is that Wimber's views on healing have remained the same between the late 1970s and today. This is not entirely the case. I see a growing trend towards embracing 'theodicy' in Wimber's theology. By 'theodicy' I mean the whole question concerning why a God of love allows people to suffer evil. One of the main reasons for this has been Wimber's traumatic treatment for throat cancer. This experience has resulted in some very honest and realistic reflections on the place of sickness and suffering in the Christian life ('it either makes you bitter or it makes you better,' he often says), and on the 'not yet' dimension of the kingdom ('in the healing ministry we are to borrow from tomorrow'). Wimber's recent teaching series on *Trials, Testing and Suffering* highlights some of these developments, yet Percy does not interact with this material at all. Nor does he interact with Wimber's recent testimonies (many of which have been reproduced in the national and international Christian media) concerning the way in which his cancer has matured his perspective. All we get is a footnote on p 180 in which Percy says,

> However, we should note that Wimber has changed some of his views on healing, following his throat cancer in 1993.

Percy ends his book with a poem by Donald Davie called 'Ordinary God' (an oxymoron as startling as the phrase 'sophisticated fundamentalist'). I would like to end this chapter with a poem written by R S Thomas. It is entitled *The Kingdom*, and it sums up Wimber's theology perfectly. As you read it, notice how Thomas delays the ending of each thought until the beginning of the following line, creating that same sense of suspended promise which is so often true of the 'not yet' of the kingdom. Notice the realism concerning sickness and poverty (features of Wimber's theology too), and yet the optimistic note of faith in the Lord who heals. For me, this sonnet forms a fitting expression of my appreciation for John Wimber and for his fruitful, kingdom ministry to us in Great Britain:

THE KINGDOM

It's a long way off but inside it
There are quite different things going on;
Festivals at which the poor man
Is king and the consumptive is
Healed; mirrors in which the blind look
At themselves and love looks at them
Back; and industry is for mending
The bent bones and the minds fractured
By life. It's a long way off, but to get
There takes no time and admission
Is free, if you will purge yourself
Of desire, and present yourself with
Your need only and the simple offering
Of your faith, green as a leaf.[13]

Notes

[1] It is interesting to look at the footnotes in Percy's book. When Percy argues that John Wimber believes in the inerrancy of Scripture, he refers in a footnote to one passage of Wimber's writing and teaching in order to justify this remark. The quotation in question is from *The Dynamics of Spiritual Growth* (London: Hodder, 1990, p 29):

I realised that the Bible was written in such a manner that to reject one part was to reject it all. This was a power point, a discovery that put me on the narrow path to salvation.

I can find absolutely no reference to biblical inerrancy in these words. Wimber is simply combatting the tired old view that the narratives contained in Luke/Acts have less authority than the didactic parts (eg, the New Testament epistles). This absurd perspective leads to the creation of a canon within the canon, with some parts of the Bible deemed less relevant and binding than others. Wimber's view is that the Bible is equally authoritative in all its parts, and that the narratives which describe the supernatural acts of God are as relevant as, say, the Sermon on the Mount. It is a sobering thought that this view results in a higher view of Scripture than that of the reformed evangelicals who oppose Wimber (and who think their view of Scripture is higher than anyone's!).

[2] Chapter 1 of *Power Evangelism* is entitled, 'The Kingdom of God' (pp 13–27). This is Wimber's starting point. In Chapter Two, where the whole notion of 'power encounters' is introduced, the concept is always subsumed under the overarching theme of the kingdom of God (particularly the biblical portrayal of the battle of the kingdoms). Note Wimber's comment on p 16 (totally ignored by Percy):

> While signs and wonders are what many visitors first notice about our church life, my understanding and experience of them come from an investigation of the kingdom of God – not out of a thirst for the supernatural.

[3] James D G Dunn, *Jesus and the Spirit. A Study of the Religious and Charismatic Experience of Jesus and the First Christians as Reflected in the New Testament* (London: SCM Press, 1975). Dunn frequently refers to the consciousness of charismatic power in the mind of Jesus, Paul and the early Christians. Of Jesus he writes:

> Jesus believed that he cast out demons by the power of God. Here, coming to clear expression, is *Jesus' consciousness of spiritual power, the visible evidence of the power of God flowing through him to overcome other superhuman power, evil power, to restore and make whole* (p 47).

In one sentence alone, Dunn refers to 'power' four times! But he is careful always to link it (as does Wimber) with the kingdom:

> So far as Jesus was concerned, the exercise of this power was *evidence that the longed-for kingdom of God had already come upon his hearers*; his exorcisms demonstrated that the last days were already present (p 47).

In both quotations above, the italics are Dunn's not mine.

[4] The seminal work on the Holy Spirit in the letters of Paul: *God's Empowering Presence*, by Gordon Fee (Peabody, MS: Hendrickson, 1994). See p 4 for Fee's explanation of his title:

> In keeping with Paul's Old Testament roots, the presence of God by the Spirit also meant for Paul the powerful and *empowering* presence of God. We are not left on our own as far as our relationship with God is concerned; neither are we left on our own to 'slug it out in the trenches', as it were, with regard to the Christian life. Life in the present is empowered by the God who dwells among us and in us. As the personal presence of God, the Spirit is not merely some 'force' or 'influence'. The living God is a God of power; and by the Spirit the power of the living God is present with us and for us.

This is surely incontrovertible, and indeed no different from the teaching consistently given by John Wimber over nearly two decades.

[5] G Fee, *God's Empowering Presence*, p 1.

[6] I think Percy overestimates the extent to which songs written by members of the Vineyard churches can be called 'Wimber's songs' and therefore an index into Wimber's 'ideology'. I would baulk at the thought of anyone using the songs written by members of my church as an index into my theological and ideological values! That would be an insult to their individuality and creativity apart from anything else.

[7] One of Percy's complaints is that the Vineyard songs reflect no liturgical or seasonal scheme in their ordering (p 62). He then cites Wesley in a footnote on p 177. This citation comes from the preface to the 1877 edition of *Collected Hymns*:

> The hymns are not carelessly jumbled together, but carefully arranged under proper heads, according to the experience of real Christians.

Percy might like to know that the 100 hymns and songs in *Let Your Glory Fall* are carefully arranged under proper heads (petitions from the *Lord's Prayer*), and in a manner which reflects 'the experience of real Christians'. But even if they had not, where is it written in stone that hymns must be arranged into seasonal, thematic, liturgical sections? That seems to me to be an Anglican prejudice rather than a theological requirement.

[8] *Let Your Glory Fall*, p 86.

[9] *Let Your Glory Fall*, p 94.

[10] *Let Your Glory Fall*, p 110.

[11] I deliberately use this phrase, 'the power of love' and 'the love of power' because it is used by Tom Smail in his essay on 'The Cross and the Spirit' in *Charismatic Renewal* (SPCK: London, 1993). This book addressed many important and urgent issues in renewal theology, issues which reoccur in Percy's book. The problem is that Percy tackles them without taking into account the changes in Wimber's theology and praxis since the beginning of the decade. I would also have to add that he addresses them with less theological acumen than the authors of *Charismatic Renewal* – Andrew Walker, Tom Smail & Nigel Wright. This is particularly visible in Percy's use of the Bible. Notice the footnote on p 174 where he says that John's version of 'the Great Commission' occurs in John 18:34,35 and 19:21–24. That is wrong! It occurs in John 15:16 and John 20:19–23.

[12] At the Harrogate Conference (Healing '95) – at which, incidentally, one member of my church was healed of chronic arthritis – John Wimber shared the platform with Francis MacNutt, a Roman Catholic. Francis' main address on the second evening was wholly devoted to unity between the different Christian denominations. This kind of overt ecumenism is hardly a characteristic of sectarian fundamentalism! Most Protestant fundamentalists arrogantly and sinfully regard Catholicism as a work of the devil!

[13] R S Thomas, *Later Poems. 1972–1982* (London: MacMillan, 1972, p 35).

CHAPTER EIGHT

John Holmes

Canon John Holmes (b. 1942) is Diocesan Missioner for the Anglican diocese of Ripon, which stretches from South Leeds to the Tees and covers parts of West and North Yorkshire. He has been in his present post since 1993 after serving most of his ministry in Leeds, including thirteen-and-a-half years in the inner city as vicar of St. Luke's, Holbeck and six-and-a-half years as vicar of the suburban parish of St James, Manston. He is author of When I am Weak *(Darton, Longman and Todd, 1992).*

John Wimber and Fr Kenneth Whitfield, an Anglo-Catholic parish priest whose ministry I encountered in the early 1970s, may seem to have little in common. However, they were both important teachers to me in the whole area of healing. Putting their approaches together was one of the challenges I was to face and wrestle with, and for which I owe much to both men.

The story begins with Fr Whitfield. My way into the healing ministry, like my way into the Christian faith, was an Anglo-Catholic one, and in the healing ministry Fr Whitfield was my first teacher. He was vicar of St Margaret's, Leeds, and around 1970 he began a monthly service of prayer for healing with the laying on of hands. It took place at 3.00pm on a Saturday afternoon. Keen supporters of Leeds United needed to set a high priority on healing to come!

At the time I was serving my second curacy in the parish of Adel in north Leeds, I lived on a large housing estate at Tinshill close by Cookridge Hospital, the regional centre for the treatment of cancer. My work in the parish included a part-time chaplaincy in the hospital, and it was there that my concern for the healing ministry developed.

But I had a big problem. I did not really believe healing could happen today in the way it seemed to be happening in the New Testament, especially in the ministry of Jesus. Of course, I believed in prayer for the sick, and I knew from my hospital chaplaincy work that positive attitudes in patients could help the healing process. I saw that for myself. The psychosomatic basis of sickness was being recognised more and more, and so I came to see the church's ministry of healing as assisting those positive attitudes in people which could aid their recovery. I came to see my ministry as a chaplain in that light too, but expecting a direct healing in answer to prayer was both beyond my experience and my theology.

It was there that Fr Whitfield helped me. An experienced parish priest, he seemed to embody a sane and sound approach to the whole subject. He had been taught to pray for the sick with the laying on of hands and anointing (when appropriate) as I had been; but after a number of years he came to believe that the traditional ministry of healing should have a higher profile in the life of the church. So he began his monthly healing services. I heard him talk about them. I attended one. He even invited me to preach at one. My pilgrimage in healing was developing.

In 1973 I was appointed vicar of St. Luke's Beeston Hill[1], an inner-city parish in Leeds with a small, loyal congregation serving a neighbourhood in the midst of considerable redevelopment. 'Our dear friend Luke the doctor' (Col 4:14) seemed an appropriate patron for a priest with an increasing concern for the healing ministry, and within a short while I had begun to put into effect some of the lessons Fr Whitfield had taught me. The first healing service I arranged was a very quiet affair: a said celebration of the eucharist one midweek evening with a short address and the laying on of hands for those desiring prayer. This soon became a monthly service and a small congregation gathered regularly for it.

In October 1974 a visitor to the parish had a big impact on the church's ministry of healing. He was Brother Jeremy Platt from the Community of the Resurrection in Mirfield. He preached and shared in the laying on of hands at our monthly healing service. A larger than usual congregation gathered. Jeremy drew not just on the riches of the sacramental approach to healing but on his experience of the charismatic renewal as well. He conveyed a confidence in ministry which drew people to the vicarage (where he was staying overnight) the morning after the service. On the afternoon before the service we had prayed together with a mother for her young child. The healing she experienced (attested later by doctors) became a talking point in church and the wider community. Expectations were raised and attendances at the monthly healing services grew. More began to report an improvement in their condition after prayer, and others a renewed faith and commitment in their lives as Christians. As years passed, the healing services continued within the context of a midweek evening eucharist; many came for the laying on of hands with prayer, the ministry led by myself, colleagues and a few senior lay leaders.

I first heard about John Wimber through my curate, Chris Lane. In 1984 he had attended the Westminster Conference led by John Wimber and his team. It was a deeply-transforming experience for him. He returned with a fresh vision for his ministry. As we talked over the conference, he told me that he had often been awed in the past by one speaker or another, but as he listened to John Wimber he was awed even more – not by him – but by God. I resolved to attend the 1985 conference in Sheffield City Hall. Rosemary, my wife, a new colleague and his wife, and a lay leader came with me.

It all seemed a long way from St. Margaret's, Leeds at 3.00pm on a Saturday afternoon in the early 1970s. At St Margaret's the reverent hush of the congregation, the aroma of incense from last Sunday's worship, the gentle organ music had provided the setting for the healing ministry. But in Sheffield City Hall there was a joyful and enthusiastic buzz in the large crowd which had gathered – and at times other sounds too, that were more disturbing! I was not sure what I had arrived at or what I was letting myself in for. The very size of the gathering filling me with a sense of both expectation and trepidation. But the quality of the worship and the impact of John Wimber's teaching helped me to be attentive to the Holy Spirit and to what God was showing me. From all that I heard and saw and experienced over those days, three things stood out:

First, there was the truth that the ministry of healing is for the whole body of Christ. Of course, I had heard that before and sometimes had seen it in operation in meetings where we had been encouraged to pray for one another. But the experience at Sheffield wrote this large in my understanding. The way people prayed in informal groups all over the City Hall was a striking witness to this, as was the way John Wimber's team worked in an enabling way. Here particular gifts in ministry were used together in a collaborative style to serve the person being prayed for. The 'one-man-band' approach seemed truly dead, with all its attendant dangers of focusing the source of healing on the person who is ministering rather than on God. If this could be the danger of some forms of personal Pentecostal healing ministries, it could also be the danger of locating the ministry exclusively in the ordained priesthood. I had been alerted to this before, by an Irish parishioner who told me, 'Father, your hands are healing hands!' Now I saw how a biblical model for shared ministry in healing could be worked out in practice.

Second, I saw healing prayer in a new light, too. Here the praying for those in need was done not only in collaboration with one another, but also in collaboration with God. This may seem an obvious point, but how often prayer for healing can be *our* prayer offered in *our* way in the name of God without much reference at the time to how God's purposes would be fulfilled. Praying with your eyes open, and seeing what was happening seemed such an obvious thing to do in the healing ministry, but we only started doing it after we had been to Sheffield. The five-step healing model:

The interview 'What's the matter?'

The diagnostic decision 'Why?'

The prayer selection 'How do we pray?'

The prayer engagement 'How are we doing?'

The post prayer direction 'What next?'

We found a practical tool and still do. Throughout, the emphasis is on waiting on God – and seeking his direction as he gives guidance in the work of ministry.

Third, we saw the close relationship between healing and evangelism. 'Preach the gospel, heal the sick' was the apostolic commission. We saw how that was being worked out across the world today, and could be in our own situation. John Wimber did not teach in my hearing a simplistic belief that healing always resulted from prayer. In fact it was from him I first heard the suggestion that Timothy suffered from a timid tummy (1 Timothy 5:23). Nor in my hearing (or reading) did he teach that healing invariably accompanied evangelism, but he gave many examples of how proclamation of the gospel had been witnessed to by God adding 'his witness to theirs by performing all kinds of miracles and wonders and by distributing the gifts of the Holy Spirit according to his will' (Hebrews 2:4 GNB).

Back in the parish we began to put these lessons to work. We extended the healing ministry in the life of the church and community. We recruited and trained a team of more than two dozen lay people to share in the healing ministry. We learnt to minister together waiting on God and using the particular gifts and insights of different people.

We moved the main focus of the ministry to our Sunday morning worship. We had experienced this the weekend after the conference in Sheffield, when one of the teams John Wimber brought over from the USA visited our parish. A young pastor from Chicago preached on 'good news for the poor' and at the end of the service I joined with visiting team members in offering ministry. I had been frankly unsure how all this would work in the setting of our conventional Sunday morning Parish Communion, but in the event my anxieties were ill-founded. The team members ministered with great sensitivity, many knew the healing touch of God and, as one of the most traditional of church members said afterwards to me, 'I have never sensed the presence of God more strongly in this church.' Opportunities for prayer and ministry became regular occasions then on Sunday mornings towards the end of the service after Communion.

And the ministry spread beyond the church walls. In ordinary homes and elsewhere in the neighbourhood people began to step out more in faith seeking God's healing and peace for those in particular need. On November 5th a few weeks after the Sheffield Conference, a community bonfire was held near a local community centre. As the fire burned and parkin was eaten, I noticed two church members chatting to one of the people serving refreshments. She told them of her need for healing. The next minute, without any fuss or self-conscious display they were quietly praying and ministering to her. And the fire burned on . . .

To this day the healing ministry has a significant place in the life and work of that inner-city parish. But in the autumn of 1986 – a year after the Sheffield Conference and thirteen-and-a-half years after first moving to south Leeds – I became vicar of St James, Manston in the large suburban parish of

Cross Gates in east Leeds. This was not only a very different neighbourhood but also a very different church.

With an Anglo-Catholic tradition of worship and ministry, it was not immediately clear to me how all that I had learnt from John Wimber could be incorporated into the rich sacramental life of St. James' Church. The healing ministry of the church was alive and active, but it was always exercised by the clergy in a personal ministry of prayer, laying on of hands and anointing. Yet a large hospital stood at one end of the parish and, though it was served by its own chaplaincy team, many parishioners including a good number of churchgoers worked there. This gave the congregation a very practical concern for healing and a ready response when I was invited to arrange a course on 'Healing and Wholeness' in my first Lent in the parish.

'The ministry of healing is an enormous and difficult subject,' I had written in promoting the course. 'What I hope to do through the Lent course is to look at healing and suffering from a biblical standpoint and then see what that implies for the church's ministry of healing today. The course will be practical . . . '

It exceeded my expectations. Between forty and fifty attended the four meetings I led, and about eighty people came to the Healing Eucharist that concluded it. Of particular significance to me was the comment of someone from a Pentecostal background, hearing of my explanation of the healing ministry based on John Gunstone's helpful criterion of pastoral care, sacramental signs and charismatic power in Chapter Three of *The Lord is Our Healer* (London: Hodders 1986). I had spoken of the care of the sick, visiting and befriending, counselling, the Eucharist, laying on of hands, anointing, absolution, the prayer group and personal ministry responding to the Spirit as all belonging to the church's armoury in exercising this ministry. He commented, 'I'd no idea the church had so much to offer.'

But the Lent course was only the beginning. We were

learning at Manston those lessons Fr Whitfield had taught me many years before but the contribution of John Wimber was only just beginning to make itself felt. A new openness to the Spirit had to be allied to a devotion to Jesus Christ that many already had in the congregation. It was not easy for those who had a high regard for the ministry of the ordained priesthood to believe that the ministry was for them too. Prayer was usually seen to be formal, rather than informal and there was a deep reticence at sharing personal experience. The picture began to change but only slowly and the ministry of healing changed only slowly too.

A monthly midweek Eucharist with the laying on of hands and anointing was begun some six months after the Lent course in 1987. It was not until 1992 that the opportunity for prayer and ministry was offered at the Sunday Eucharist, but the move towards that flowed from a growing concern from within the congregation and not just from the leadership of the clergy. And when the ministry was offered (in the Lady Chapel at the end of the service) it was exercised by groups of lay people who had been recruited and trained using the five steps we had first learnt from John Wimber. The desire to integrate insights from John Wimber into a sacramental approach to the healing ministry had gone a long way.

Since 1986 John Wimber has faced much personal suffering in his life, not least in his own fight with cancer. Reflection on all this has led to some important developments in his teaching. Engaging in parish ministry, which I did from 1966 to 1993, means a continual encounter with the suffering of others, which tends to militate against simplistic approaches to healing as containing all the answers. The mystery of suffering is a constant companion. Only the full richness of a healing ministry that is pastoral, sacramental and charismatic can adequately serve the needs of the sick, the suffering and the disturbed. I remain deeply grateful to John Wimber for the contribution he made to my own understanding and exercise of this ministry which has enabled me to seek an integration of all that is good in different approaches.

The focus though must always be on the kingdom of God we are called to announce, proclaim and seek. It was Hans Küng, the Roman Catholic theologian, who described the kingdom of God as 'creation healed' – the restoration of all things in Christ. As St Paul wrote:

> For in him God in all his fullness chose to dwell, and through him to reconcile all things to himself, making peace through the shedding of his blood on the cross – all things, whether on earth or in heaven (Colossians 1:19,20).

My work as a diocesan missioner has only reinforced in me the belief that healing and evangelism go together. Christ's call to the seventy to 'heal the sick there and say, ''The kingdom of God has come close to you'' ' (Luke 10.9) remains at the heart of my faith and experience. Sharing in a recent mission in Cardiff – a venture that drew together Christians of a wide spectrum of tradition – I saw how the proclamation of the gospel can be accompanied by works of healing and restoration. A memorable healing service in a Methodist church demonstrated that. But it is important to stress both sides of the equation, for healing needs evangelism, too. Healing without evangelism sells the gospel short, as if Jesus just came to make things a little better rather than a whole lot different.

Sometimes John Wimber or his followers are criticised for being more concerned with signs and wonders than the proclamation of the gospel. Voices have been raised recently over a tendency among some who would claim John Wimber as inspiration for an over-concern with the unusual, sensational action of the Spirit, rather than the deeper, longer lasting and usually more hidden work within. It is vital that it is the Spirit of the Crucified One and not the consumer spirit which leads us in mission and ministry.

Every now and again I listen to the story of John Wimber's

personal pilgrimage, the first talk given at the early Wimber conferences. The humour and the honesty reveal a man who once having been found by the love of God is determined to share that knowledge and experience with family, friends and as many people as possible. It is probably John Wimber's work on how the work of evanglism can be most effectively exercised by the church which will be his greatest legacy. A church truly attentive to the Spirit, using the gifts and ministries of all, trained and mobilised for mission – if we see such a church more often in Western society today, John Wimber has certainly made a significant contribution to that picture.

Notes

[1] From 1976 it became the enlarged parish of St Luke's, Holbeck.

CHAPTER NINE

Peter Lawrence

Peter H. Lawrence (b. 1947) is Team Rector of Canford Magna, Dorset. He and his wife Carol, with their three daughters, moved to Dorset from a parish in inner-city Birmingham. Peter is a regular conference speaker and well-established author. Amongst his most popular books are The Hot Line *(Kingsway, 1990),* Doing What Comes Supernaturally *(Kingsway, 1992) and* Signs and Blunders *(Monarch, 1994).*

In the summer of 1984 I read David Watson's book, *Fear No Evil*, about his struggle with terminal cancer. In it I read of a man called John Wimber who flew over from America especially to pray for him. David died on February 18th, 1984. Soon after I'd finished the book I was approached by a Baptist friend.

'Are you coming to the Wimber conference on Signs and Wonders?' he asked.

I wasn't much into conferences then, I wasn't particularly keen on Americans, and the track record I knew about Wimber didn't seem too impressive. I didn't go.

Afterwards some local clergy who'd been to the conference held a follow-up lunch and I sneaked in. I've been to many ministers' lunches. Normally we use them as an opportunity for moaning to sympathetic ears about our unresponsive congregations. But this was different. The conversation was awesome. I was gobsmacked. I arrived late, took my place at a table and heard a well-known minister friend sharing his testimony.

'The Lord gave me this word,' he began. 'A lady here with twisted fallopian tubes. She came out the front. We laid hands on her, she fell over and she went back to the hospital – completely healed.'

I wanted to ask questions but others were desperate to share their stories.

'Fifteen men in our prison have been converted,' interjected the prison chaplain who was among us. 'All I did was ask God to come and – bang! Power. Shaking. Healing. Changed lives. It's beginning to affect the whole prison.'

'I visited a couple who weren't Christians,' said a lady before I had time to take in the prison story. 'He had an ulcer. I laid on hands. Power came. All the pain went. She had a bad headache and 'flu. I laid on hands and she felt instantly better. They were both amazed. "Before you go," said the man, "the dog's got a bad leg." Guess what?'

I guessed. I normally have plenty to say but not at this luncheon. I felt I had nothing to offer. I needed to go to such a conference to see for myself. In autumn 1985 there was a 'Signs and Wonders' in Sheffield. My wife Carol was expecting our third child but I had to be in Sheffield. I hope she understood. I think she did.

I sat right by the exit on the end of the row. I wasn't too keen on other people hearing 'words of knowledge' about my life. I was fascinated but I was scared. I had one eye on the stage and one eye on the way out. At least I was there.

In due course this rotund American began to speak. He looked just like Santa Claus from the movie. Not what I expected at all. He didn't shout at us. He was funny. He was laid back. And above all else he was fat. Clearly he had a problem. Probably a fast-food American problem. But it meant one thing to me. If God can use this man maybe he can also use me.

I prepared myself for the hype. I knew after the stories there would be ministry. 'We'll have a ten minute break,' Wimber said, 'I need to go to the loo.' What a let down. This was definitely different.

He returned – went to the mike – invited us to stand and without a word of preparation prayed, 'Come Holy Spirit.' Then he waited in silence and watched. So did I. Slowly people began to weep. It spread right around the auditorium. 'God is weeping for his church,' said John. 'God wants his church back.'

During the week I saw people healed. I experienced demons cast out. 'Words of knowledge' were given and claimed and more were healed. My unproven prejudices and my socks were blown away. I'd been a Christian since 1962. I knew this stuff was in the book. I'd always believed in it before, theoretically. Now for the first time in my life I was seeing it, experiencing it and feeling it. This was God. This was truth. I simply had to go home and try it for myself, just as they'd taught us in the seminars.

So I did – every week for a year until God began to come in power. Our churchwarden was in pain and agony through trapped sciatic nerves and torn muscles. He fell over at the laying on of hands, twitched about, and stood up completely healed. An unbeliever shook all over, fell to the ground, and came up believing. A teenager, virtually blind, manifested a demon which I cast out in the name of Jesus. Immediately his sight was fully restored. Having seen all these things I can never be the same again. To God be all the glory.

John Wimber has always been plagued with sickness. In his early twenties doctors gave him no more than a year to live. 'Not always a precise science,' comments John now sixty-two. Despite his own struggle with ill-health his travelling, preaching and ministering to the needy though being costly has always been given freely.

A friend of mine approached John following a long session of teaching and ministry and asked for help. 'Of course,' he replied.

'I'm troubled by demons,' she continued.

'I can see that,' said John and proceeded to look straight into her eyes. At the word of command in Jesus' name there was an explosion in her head, more power than she'd ever experienced before came upon her, and more demons seemed to leave in a minute than had previously left in several hours during ministry from me. Throughout the four-day conference John was on stage playing the keyboard, speaking or ministering most of the time but still found time to pray for over sixty individuals who asked for his help. And all this despite suffering from a bad heart.

In 1988 I was privileged to be a member of the ministry team which accompanied John and Carol to South Africa. When the conference began in Johannesburg John met us outside the hotel at 8.30am to check everything was OK. When we arrived at the National Exhibition Centre there he was seeing to his keyboard alongside the other musicians (not so much transported by the Spirit as a faster car). He spoke and led ministry for most of the day. During the one session he was missing. Archbishop Bill Burnett asked me if I knew where he was. 'Probably having a kip,' I suggested, 'he's not that fit you know.' I was wrong. The only time he was missing he was having deep discussions with Martyn Smith about starting a Vineyard in Manchester.

In the evening meeting John invited people with serious conditions to come forward for prayer. My friend William struggled to hide a limp wherever we went so I asked him afterwards why he'd not gone forward. 'I have received some prayer,' he replied, 'but it's not that straightforward. I was born with a malformation. Part of the leg never grew properly. It needs much more than being lengthened by a couple of inches.'

At 10.30pm we began to make our way out of the hall. These were long days. As we did so we bumped into Jeff and Nancy from Anaheim who were walking in front of John and Carol Wimber.

'Hey Jeff and Nancy,' I yelled in an awful American accent. 'How ya doin'?'

'Oh terribly well I think,' replied Nancy imitating an English polo player. 'Absolutely super.'

I sensed an opportunity. 'Can you guys lengthen legs?' I asked – still in jocular fashion

'Yeh, we can sometimes do legs,' said Jeff.

'My friend William wants to be taller,' I said, 'on one side.' My friend William gave me an embarrassed British look. I sensed I was in for a rough time when we returned to our room. At this point John and Carol caught up with us.

'Peter Wagner can lengthen legs, can't he?' I enquired of John who despite looking tired smiled.

'God has used him a few times in this way, yeh!'

There was a pause. A moment's hesitation.

'OK Carol. Let's have a go.' There was no escape for William.

Despite the hour, the length of the day and the condition of the heart, they 'had a go' there and then. Jeff and Nancy sat William down on the cold concrete floor. Carol Wimber did the laying on of hands while John gave out a few instructions. They didn't appear to be following the 'Wimber model' I'd read about in his books.

All kinds of power seemed to come on William. He shook, he twitched, he jerked and even sweated despite the cold autumnal May evening. John and Carol gave him their full attention for some time.

Afterwards William was fully appreciative of my efforts.

'You rat, Lawrence!' he said with a cheeky grin. 'It was wonderful.'

No! William wasn't healed physically but he was blessed emotionally to the point of being released into dance during the worship from then on. He'd always been too self-conscious before. John's sacrificial giving of himself and his time meant a lot to all of us on the British team who witnessed the incident.

When I returned home from South Africa I began writing my first book. I decided early on to send a copy of the relevant chapter to everyone mentioned in it so that permission and opinions could be sought and facts checked. It was a long and tedious task for my wonderful secretary.

In Chapter Two I briefly mentioned my attendance at a John Wimber conference in 1985. That was all. My secretary sent a duplicated letter and a copy of the chapter to John. In the twinkling of an eye we received back three sides of A4 close-typed comments on what I had written. I still have them. He even apologised for writing them to me uninvited. Busy clergy will appreciate this loving and sacrificial response from a man who sometimes receives 200 letters a day.

One of our ministers' fraternal visited Anaheim in the late eighties. At first we all had difficulty believing the report he brought back. It was something way beyond anything any of us had ever met before, but his insistence and own credibility persuaded us to accept his assessment.

'John Wimber,' he said, 'actually loves the people in his own congregation.'

I hope I will be forgiven for saying I've always regarded John Wimber as a man who stumbles upon staggering truth. He came to the Bible with the prejudicial presuppositions of a saxophone player – ie, none at all! What he read was what he believed, and what he believed was what he practised. He'd led many people to Christ before he went to theological college and was told that was not the way it is, and possibly not even the way it was.

Jesus proclaimed the kingdom, healed the sick and cast out demons in the power of the Holy Spirit – so John Wimber did the same. *And it worked*. Why shouldn't it? What a staggering truth to stumble upon! He has embarrassed some of us who have been influenced by liberal lies like the little boy who saw through the emperor's suit of clothes. We have been compelled to move from liberal to liberated theology. It is true. The Lord has risen. Hallelujah!

When we Anglicans first heard and experienced Wimber we were refreshed, renewed and revived. It was not just that he didn't shout at us and tell us off. It was not just that God demonstrated signs and wonders through him without hype or hysteria. It was that he successfully argued from Scripture how signs and wonders are an integral part of the coming of the kingdom of God. Interestingly this is not new to theologians. The liberal Rudolf Bultmann in his New Testament theology; the Roman Catholic Raymond Brown in his New Testament expositions; the evangelical George Ladd in his book on Jesus and the kingdom, have all argued that signs and wonders in the New Testament are seen as the evidence of an advance on the kingdom of Satan by the coming in power of the kingdom of God. But, like the miracles themselves, our familiarity with them had bred a kind of contempt, that is, until we began to experience them for ourselves. We probably had not even believed in the kingdom of Satan as a reality before. But now, following what we had seen with our eyes, what we had looked at and our hands had touched, when John opened up the Scriptures to us, our hearts burned within us.

John Wimber's book, *Power Healing*, has sold many times more than the average Christian paperback, but John was deeply hurt by the critics at the time.

'How can anyone write a book on Christian healing without mentioning the Cross?' they asked.

For several months, wherever John went he kept muttering, 'Would that my enemy would write a book,' and frequently reminded us how often he preached on the Cross at home.

And yet, in his own way, John had stumbled on another truth. There is another book out that doesn't link physical healing to the Cross or the atonement – the New Testament. I know it can be argued. The Pentecostals have been arguing it all century. But the New Testament doesn't argue it. Instead it shows how Jesus and his disciples healed the sick in the power of the Holy Spirit, with the authority of God the Father. John, in describing his experience adequately supported by scriptural references, and omitting what the New Testament has omitted, has freed us from shouting at cripples in wheelchairs to have more faith in the Cross.

As in the days of Jesus, the most vehement critics of those who preach with signs following have always been from *within* the church. Those who have found that John Wimber did not fit their presuppositions about style, personality, practice or theology have been quickest to sharpen their critical quills.

The liberals who don't believe God ever breaks into our lives with supernatural signs and wonders have looked for natural explanations and reverted frequently to cries of hype and hysteria. They obviously have not attended the same meetings I have or met the same man.

The cessationists cry 'all is demonic and deception' and end up having to say good, kingdom of God fruit is being produced by Satan and his hordes. Even if Satan does deceive us initially, the seeds he sows can only eventually grow thorns and thistles, never grapes. Such critics have caused much unnecessary fear and doubt in the church leading some to believe that life is death, white is black and the kingdoms of God and Satan are interchangeable. I prefer Wimber's more straightforward approach to Scripture and experience. When people are saved, healed or set free from demons in the name of Jesus, it is probably Jesus who is doing it.

The more fearful, who are often most afraid that anything good might happen in our churches, tend to keep their eyes on the lunatic fringe rather than on Jesus. There is frequently some cause for concern here. 'A wicked and adulterous generation asks for a miraculous sign!' (Mt 12:39). The problem is the four-day conference. Any sensational sign-seeker can pay his money and turn up just as they obviously did, but for free, in Jesus' day. The mud-slinging critic can then easily fill up his blunderbuss with ammunition from the fringe and fire at will.

But those who know John Wimber, other Vineyard pastors and their trained ministry teams, and who have taken time to visit their churches as well as their conferences will know that the criticism of 'seeking a sign' rather than the kingdom of God is unfounded.

Love of God, obedience to God and compassion for people is what motivates John. The advantage of being a 'Righteous Brother' before becoming a Christian (now much more right-eous), and at one time having three singles in the American pop music charts, (see p. 12) is that since then he has never sought the big stage, fame or fortune. He was converted from it, not to it. His love for God and people impresses all who meet him and get to know him. In his relatively fitter days he frequently spent quality time with people and placed caring for the needy high on his agenda.

The 'signs and wonders' that John teaches are connected mostly with 'power evangelism' and 'power healing'. He longs to see non-Christians saved and suffering individuals healed. His reason for holding big conferences is to teach and equip as many Christians as possible to do these things, so that God's kingdom may be advanced more quickly and effectively and the name of Jesus glorified. Anyone who accuses John of lesser motives simply does not know John Wimber.

There have, of course, been times when John has made
errors of judgment. In October 1990 many gathered at the
Docklands in London for revival to break out, having been
invited by John who was reacting to a Paul Cain prophecy.
Nothing obvious or visible of an exceptional nature took
place. Even so, the unequivocal apology which followed
later was a true mark of his Spirit-filled character. John
Wimber has made mistakes in his time but has always
been prepared to admit them publicly. To pioneer – is to
take risks – is to be fallible.

I saw John a couple of times in 1995. He'd lost eight stone
and needed a saliva spray to keep talking. He tires more
easily now. We may not see him much more in Britain.
And yet in the ministry-time John was back to equipping
the saints, ministering in the power of the Holy Spirit, just
like old times – and it was splendid.

Where do we go from here? I think, inevitably, the
removal of John Arnott and the Toronto church from the
Vineyard heralds the end of a movement and the beginning
of a denominational church. When two groups so close in
theology and practice have to part, it shows that the narrow
denominational guillotine is coming down and the pioneering spirit is over. It was always thus. Institutionalisation
enters the equation at the second generation stage and boxes
the vision in for the sake of security. But we can still learn
from John and the Vineyard and keep 'doing the stuff'. John
Wimber's gifting, anointing and calling has always been to
equip the saints. This he has done more effectively and
graciously than anyone else I have ever met, and we can
continue applying the lessons he has taught us.

I am a first generation Wimber-keenie. John has clearly
demonstrated to me how proclaiming the kingdom, healing
the sick and casting out demons are all part of the same
'Jesus package'. In the power of the Holy Spirit he has taught
me, shown me and equipped me to do it. Around the globe
God is using many others to do the same things (but much

more effectively than me). The Word of God with signs following is making many new Christian converts in other parts of the world.

At home I sense some hearts are growing colder. An interesting movement which entertained us for a while may now be passing. The church in many places is still in decline. Institutionalised Christianity amongst the middle-classes does not want to shake, rattle and roll in the aisles any more. It was only fun for a season.

But the hungry, thirsty, spiritual beggars of the world, who haven't any pride to care less about, are beginning to taste a feast. Whether it is a preparation for Jesus' return, whether it is a preparation for a new wave of persecution, or whether it is simply because God loves us, I want it. I want it for God's church in our land. I want it for my non-Christian neighbours. But most of all I want it because charismatic Christianity is biblical Christianity. It is what God has revealed to us as the 'norm' that God wants. It is what John Wimber has taught me is possible in my life, in our churches and in our land, through God's good grace.

A friend said to me recently, 'I am not charismatic by disposition or nature. I am charismatic by belief because the New Testament does not allow for any other kind of Christian.'

Two other friends shared with me how belonging to the anti-Wimber, anti-Toronto camp had led them down a slippery slope towards becoming anti-charismatic. Recognising this enabled them to stop in their tracks, to come humbly in repentance to God and receive much blessing from him.

I believe John Wimber has shown us how all Christians can be equipped by the Holy Spirit to serve Jesus Christ in biblical ways. The Spirit confirms the Word and the Word confirms the Spirit. He has demonstrated in power what God is only too willing to do for us. Our response will undoubtedly shape our destiny.

Anne Watson has always remained the best of friends with John and Carol Wimber. Even though David died she is still grateful for the way John flew over from America to pray for her husband. With all I have now seen and heard, if one day I was told I had cancer, it would be John Wimber I would want most of all to come and pray for me.

CHAPTER TEN

David Lewis

Dr David C Lewis (b. 1956) is a social anthropologist whose book Healing: Fiction, Fantasy or Fact? *(Hodder and Stoughton, 1989) presents the results of his detailed follow-up study of the results of John Wimber's* Signs and Wonders (Part II) *conference in Harrogate in 1986. In addition to some guest lecturing and freelance writing, David currently acts as an anthropological consultant for several Christian organisations. He is also personally involved in humanitarian aid activities and other forms of assistance among some of the lesser-known ethnic groups of northern Eurasia.*

'David! Quick! There's someone calling you on the phone from California!' My wife, Ruth, had a note of urgency in her voice.

I rushed out of the neighbour's caravan which I'd been using as an office and dashed across the road, wondering who could possibly be phoning me from America. It turned out to be Kevin Springer, co-author of John Wimber's book *Power Evangelism*. He explained that their next book, *Power Healing*, was about to be published and he wanted to ask if they could include an article of mine in it as an appendix.

Unknown to me, Dr John White – the Christian psychiatrist and author – had sent a copy of my article to John Wimber. I had not expected this kind of reaction when, following a suggestion by Bishop David Pytches, I had sent a copy of the article to John White for his comments. Through this circuitous process I suddenly found myself becoming not only a contributor to one of Wimber's books but also someone whose opinion was sought concerning Wimber's ministry.

It was in 1984 that I first heard of John Wimber, from the enthusiastic report of a friend of ours who had attended a conference of his in London. I was curious to see for myself what this was all about when the opportunity arose for me to attend Wimber's conference in Sheffield in 1985. However, I ended up going to that conference not only as a participant but also as a researcher. Two months previously I had started a research project for the Religious Experience Research Unit at Nottingham University and for the Alister Hardy Research Centre in Oxford.[1] When I mentioned to my boss about Wimber's Sheffield conference, he said I could take time off my other research in order to attend it – but on condition that I wrote an academic article about it afterwards! So it was that I ended up attending the conference as a 'participant-observer', using my professional training as a social anthropologist. I interviewed people about their experiences and took detailed notes of what was said and done.

In retrospect, I can also see the Lord's sense of humour in what happened to me personally. During a ministry session on the first day of the conference, I chose to remain standing while many others sat down. I was aware of the Lord's presence, but in a way similar to that which I had felt on other occasions. Suddenly John Wimber pointed in my direction and said, 'The Holy Spirit is on you.' I looked around to see who he was talking about! Noticing then that most others were sitting down, I sat down too and continued to observe what was going on.

Two days later, however, God had a surprise for me during a 'workshop' led by Blaine Cook when I was sitting with my eyes shut in an attitude of prayer. Although I was aware of the Holy Spirit's presence, my feelings were identical to those I often felt when I asked God to fill me with his Spirit. Cook asked us to stretch out our hands towards those on the stage who were receiving ministry, to 'bless' what God was doing in their lives. I did so. Afterwards one of those sitting near me remarked, 'The Holy Spirit was really on you during that session!'

'What do you mean?,' I asked, surprised at his comment. He then told me how my right hand had been shaking strongly and my head was back with my face uplifted in a manner characteristic of the activity of the Holy Spirit. I had been totally unaware of this and would have doubted his account if another man nearby had not confirmed it. God used this to help convince me that such manifestations of the Spirit could happen even to a researcher who was not actively seeking such experiences and was trying to assess the phenomena in a detached and relatively objective manner![2] On my return home that night, Ruth said to me, 'Elizabeth (a friend of ours) has been telling me about all these people who have been shaking and doing other weird things: you've not been doing anything like that, have you?'[3]

In this and other ways I became convinced that God was at work in the kind of ministry associated with John Wimber. Such a conviction could not remain merely an intellectual one, but had to influence my faith too. My own spiritual life was transformed as a result of my exposure to this kind of ministry: in many ways it was like a 're-conversion' experience, through which I came into a fresh relationship with God.

Shortly after I first became a Christian I had expected to hear God speaking to me through direct revelations or through healing people in answer to my prayers. Later, however, I had become involved with a church where people were not accustomed to such experiences. Therefore, in a subtle manner, I had become 'socialised' into not expecting God to speak directly to people or to intervene very often in their lives through 'supernatural' healings. My witnessing at first hand John Wimber's expectancy for God to give him 'words of knowledge' and to work through him in healing and deliverance helped to restore me to the kind of relationship with God which I had had at the beginning. I, too, began to expect God to use even me in this way. Therefore, if I now had to name one person (apart from Jesus) who has most profoundly influenced my spiritual life so far, without a doubt the choice would be John Wimber.

It was not until a year after the Sheffield conference, however, that I first had the opportunity to discuss with John in person about his ministry. This was at the Harrogate conference in 1986, which I was investigating in a much more comprehensive manner through detailed questionnaires and in-depth interviews.[4] Ruth and our six-month-old daughter, Bethany, came with me to visit Wimber. I was a little apprehensive about how I would get on with him. Probably sensing my unease, John's first comment to me was, 'Yes, David, God does love the English as well!' I soon loosened up!

With us at that meeting was Paul Wilcox, then a student at a Baptist college in Bristol, who was also doing some research on Wimber's ministry. Paul told us how the students at the college had read my appendix in *Power Healing* first, and on the basis of my research then decided that the rest of the book was worth reading too!

John's attitude to my research was refreshing. He told me that he did not mind what kinds of conclusions I came to, because he trusted my methodology. I was prepared to assess the evidence carefully, in as scientific a manner as possible, and to conduct detailed interviews. This contrasted with the reports on his ministry by those who gave opinions based on superficial impressions and anecdotes without attempting any systematic collection of data or analysis of what actually took place. I appreciated John's sincerity and honesty, and his willingness to let me examine his ministry because he trusted me to do it in a proper manner.

My next meeting with John was not until February 1989. In the meantime I had analysed the 1,890 usable questionnaires collected at the end of the Harrogate conference, followed up a random sample of 100 people for interviews between six months and one year after the conference, contacted medical doctors about interesting cases of healing, and written up my results for a book. I brought with me a copy of the manuscript which I gave to John, as the book was not published until later that year.

John was fascinated by some of my findings, as I had discovered aspects of his ministry which he himself had not noticed. For instance, he was surprised when I pointed out to him that those aged less than forty constituted 85% of the people responding to a highly specific 'word of knowledge', whereas the percentage dropped to 60% and 46% respectively for revelations of medium and low specificity.[5] This related also to my finding that on the whole younger people tended to report greater degrees of healing than older people.

Immediately John's fertile mind started to make connections with surveys which showed how younger people tend to be those who respond more to evangelistic campaigns such as those by Billy Graham. He was already aware that in such contexts there is a greater responsiveness among younger people, but he had not realised that this also applied to his own healing ministry.[6]

Afterwards Kevin Springer told me that John was clearly interested in what I had to say because he had given me so much of his time. Our meeting was over breakfast one Monday morning after a very intensive week. John was apparently glad to get away from his telephone, which had been constantly ringing as Vineyard pastors around America were phoning to ask about what had been going on at the 'Spiritual Warfare' conference in Anaheim that previous week. The conference had been specially extended over the weekend in order that more people could benefit from the ministry of Paul Cain. This was the first time John had invited Paul to minister at one of his conferences. That Monday morning John told me how he himself had never previously seen such a powerful operation of the gifts of the Holy Spirit of the kind he had seen manifested in Paul's ministry.

In introducing Paul at the beginning of the conference, John had described their first meeting two months previously, in December 1988. Paul had come to John with a message from the Lord, and had accurately predicted that on the day he arrived in California there would be a 'sign in the ground' confirming the message he had for John. At 3.38am that day there was indeed a 'shaking-type' earthquake in California which left no casualties. Moreover, the timing was also significant, because some of what Paul Cain had to tell John was focused around the promise in Jeremiah 33:8.[7]

I had to wait until the following October to hear about a sequel to this story which was very relevant to me. In retrospect, I believe the Lord had allowed me to be ignorant of something else which Paul had predicted so that my own actions would be done more on the basis of faith – without relying on Paul Cain's confirmation.

Towards the end of 1988 I had begun to do some research on the conflict between Armenia and Azerbaidzhan over Nagorno Karabakh. That December I would have been in that region itself had not the Soviet authorities cancelled visits by foreign tourists to a region which had become politically volatile. When I then heard about the major earthquake which occurred that month in northern Armenia, my immediate question was, 'Why, Lord?' (Why was it at this particular time, and why in Armenia?) I felt in my spirit that it had something to do with the conflict over Karabakh about which I had been researching.

Immediately the Lord brought to my mind some passages in the prophecy of Amos. Suddenly I realised how the contemporary situation in Armenia was very similar to that of Israel at the time of Amos. Both nations were supposed to be God's people, but their conduct was no better than that of their neighbours. Externally they were concerned about expanding their territory to the east but internally they were full of corruption. Two years after Amos gave his prophecy, an earthquake occurred in Israel of such a magnitude that its severity was cited by Zechariah some four centuries later (Amos 1:1; Zechariah 14:5).

I shared with a number of other Christian leaders the insights which I felt the Lord had given me, in order to gain their confirmation or otherwise about whether or not these understandings were indeed from God. Eventually, in April 1989, I felt I could delay no longer. I wrote a letter to the Catholicos (head) of the Armenian Apostolic Church in Etchmiadzin, sending it by registered mail, and sent similar letters to other Armenian Christian leaders elsewhere in the world. To each of them I explained that I realised that events like the earthquake are difficult for anybody to interpret, but nevertheless I wanted humbly to offer them the insights which I believed God had given me. With the letter I sent a six-page article entitled 'Armenia and Amos' in which I set out what I felt God had shown me. It concluded by stating that I believed the Armenians needed to repent of the corruption in their own midst and also to love their enemies and to pray for those who had persecuted them.

None of those Armenian Christian leaders ever replied to me. Over the following six months after sending the letter I began to wonder whether or not I had really heard from God. That October I attended a conference on 'Worship' in Brighton, where John Wimber was one of the principal speakers. He started off by talking about what had been happening in the Vineyard movement and about Paul Cain's visit to him the previous December. I had already in February heard how Paul had accurately predicted the earthquake in California, but John now added a further detail. I sat riveted to my seat as John continued his account by remarking that Paul also mentioned that on the day after he left California 'there would be a much more major earthquake elsewhere in the world which would be God's judgment on his people in that place'.

At the end of that session I hurried forward to catch John. He confirmed what I knew already in my heart, that the earthquake in question was indeed the one in Armenia. The next issue of the Vineyard magazine *Equipping the Saints* also confirmed this.[8]

My head was reeling. Here at last, through Paul Cain, I had a confirmation from the Lord about what I had communicated to the Armenian Christian leaders. John Wimber was the human agent through whom I received this information at the time when it was appropriate for me.

Naturally such ideas about why God might allow certain earthquakes can be controversial in some Christian circles. I had already shared some of these thoughts with leaders of an interdenominational Christian mission organisation for whom I was doing the research on the Nagorno Karabakh situation. Probably this added to the impression they were beginning to form of me as a rather 'extreme' charismatic!

In January 1988 the Lord had shown me clearly that he wanted me to help this organisation, so in April that year we sold our house in Leeds and moved south to Kent. However, my first priority over the summer had to be the completion of my book about John Wimber's Harrogate conference, after which I could begin the other kind of research. Of course, the very fact that I was writing such a book and talking about some of my findings also contributed to my image of being somewhat 'radical' on such issues.

Things came to a head in October 1990 when we got thrown out of the mission. This was precipitated by my getting involved in a ministry of deliverance for a man who had become a Christian from a Muslim background but still had problems in his life. The following spring the mission's general director phoned me up, apologised for what they had done and asked for my forgiveness. In retrospect, I could see how the Lord had used that experience to make me available to help a wide variety of other ministries as well as having the flexibility to pursue opportunities which the Lord was already opening up for me elsewhere.

Nevertheless, the traumatic manner in which we had been expelled from the mission did raise many immediate questions about the next steps we should take. At that time a good friend whose counsel I respect suggested that I should write and tell John Wimber about what had happened. I greatly appreciated the encouragement and helpful advice which he offered. An unanticipated extra blessing was his sending us a gift of £300. Just once before, when we first joined the mission, he had also sent us a donation. Both of these unexpected gifts came at times when we particularly needed that kind of encouragement and support.

Since then we have been in contact now and again about matters such as a Russian translation of *Power Healing*. However, I have been reluctant to contact John too much because I am aware that he has many other demands on his time. Sometimes we have met while John has been in England, most recently at the New Wine convention in 1995. Each time I have appreciated his warmth and friendship. My respect for him continues to grow as I see him continuing to minister in a Christ-like manner, combining humility with a courage to speak frankly about sensitive issues – but also expressed with wisdom and a compassion for others.

In some ways John's recent struggles with illness have demonstrated his strength of character more deeply than had been shown in public during the years when he was known particularly for his healing ministry. To a large extent he has now become a respected mentor to many within the charismatic movement whose ministries, like mine, have been greatly enriched through their exposure to John's own teaching and practice. As a 'grandfather' or 'elder statesman' figure, his wisdom, advice, encouragement and (if necessary) correction have been important stabilising elements among certain charismatics – who can sometimes be prone to over-emphasise the side-effects of the Holy Spirit's ministry or the more 'spectacular' claims of certain individuals. In all the controversies which have at times surrounded the Vineyard movement (or elements within it) what shines through as a source of confidence and stability is John Wimber's own integrity and reliability.

Notes

[1] The Oxford Centre has subsequently been renamed the Religious Experience Research Centre and is located at Westminster College.

[2] In my report on the conference, I mentioned what had happened to me but couched it in academic language without admitting that I was the 'twenty-nine-year-old man who was genuinely surprised to be told half-an-hour later that during a certain time of prayer his hand had been shaking violently'. [See David Lewis 'Signs and Wonders in Sheffield' – Appendix D in John Wimber and Kevin Springer Power Healing (London: Hodder and Stoughton, 1986), p 264.]

[3] Ruth's own turn came a few days later!

[4] My findings are presented in my book Healing: Fiction, Fantasy or Fact? (London: Hodder and Stoughton, 1989).

[5] Healing: Fiction, Fantasy or Fact?, p 158.

[6] My own perspective on this statistical tendency – which is not an absolute rule by any means – compares it with biblical and con-

temporary cases of raising the dead, which also mainly involve younger people. If God chooses to raise the dead or grant physical healing, does he still have purposes for that person on this earth which require such a healing to have taken place? By contrast, there is no statistical link with age for what is often termed 'inner healing': this frequently involves repentance or forgiveness, thereby also cleaning up the person's life in preparation for heaven.

[7] Obviously, as there are only twenty-four hours in a day, the earthquake could not occur at '33.08'! Even though minor earthquakes do often occur in California, the accurate prediction of the exact day, coinciding with a significant time on that very day, is still very highly remarkable. Verse 8 reads, 'I will cleanse them from all the sin they have committed against me and will forgive all their sins of rebellion against me.'

[8] *Equipping the Saints*, Vol 3, No 4 (Fall 1989), p 5. (However, the printed account did not include the comment spoken by John at Brighton about the earthquake being a form of judgment on God's people.)

CHAPTER ELEVEN

Graham Horsley

Graham Horsley (b. 1955) is a Methodist minister presently serving South Chadderton Methodist Church in the Oldham and Saddleworth Circuit. He was formerly minister of churches in Bradford and Hull. He also works part-time for the Home Mission Division of the Methodist Church as Church Planting Development Worker. He has written the Methodist guide to planting churches – Planting New Congregations *(Methodist Publishing House, 1994). He is a member of the Challenge 2000 Steering Group and a regular speaker at 'Easter People'.*

I have seen John Wimber many times, I have received a great deal of help in my personal relationship with Christ and in my work as a Methodist minister as a result of John's ministry, but I have never spoken to him or had direct help or advice from him. My tribute to his ministry is that of one of the many thousands of Christians worldwide who have attended the conferences, read the books, listened to the tapes and somewhere along the way met with Jesus.

My first experience of a 'Signs and Wonders' conference

came as a result of a storm. It was in November 1986 when John and his team came to Harrogate. At that time I was minister of two Methodist churches in Hull and was going through a time of spiritual dryness. I could see that God was using me, but I was aware of so many ways in which I was not living up to the ideals I had set for myself. I often felt inadequate for the task facing me and weighed down by the guilt of failure, I had lost the enthusiasm in my faith which had been a vital part of my early experience of God.

Before being called to the ministry, I received the baptism in the Holy Spirit in 1973 whilst at university. My whole relationship with God was transformed, I found prayer and worship tremendously exciting and began to experience the gifts of the Holy Spirit. My call to the ministry was as a result of a very clear prophetic message, and I began training with a strong vision for what was to happen. Ten years later, the reality of ministry was very different from my naive expectations and in fact I felt further away from God than when I began. Looking back I realise that there were two problems. The first was maintaining my own spirituality under the pressure of being a Christian leader – I had neglected my personal walk with God. The second problem was that of sharing my own experience of the Holy Spirit in a church which had little experience of God moving in this way.

The Methodist church is organised in 'circuits' consisting of a group of churches (normally between ten and twenty) led by a team of ministers. This has meant that radical ideas take much longer to be absorbed into its life than in churches where a strong leader can have a powerful influence on a church. Methodism has been influenced by the charismatic movement in many ways, but it is difficult to point to individual churches which have become clearly charismatic in the way that one can in other denominations. It is difficult to lead a congregation forward following a God-given vision when next Sunday's preacher may arrive with a very different agenda. This led to a considerable amount of frustration on my part. I knew where I wanted to lead the churches in my pastoral care, but I couldn't see clearly how to go about it!

Although I could not have put it into words back in November 1986, I desperately needed to be refreshed in my relationship with God and to discover how to release others into ministering in the power of the Holy Spirit.

I received publicity for the Harrogate conference but was unsure about whether or not to attend. It was expensive, John Wimber was an American (yes – I'm prejudiced!). I had also heard conflicting stories about his ministry. Some testified to experiencing God in a new way which excited me but I had also heard rumours of excesses (usually unspecified!) that made me wonder whether or not I should become involved. A further complication was that I had for some years taken a few days off in the autumn to go backpacking, and my diary would not allow me to go to Harrogate and to go backpacking as well. I knew that I needed spiritual refreshment, but persuaded myself that a few days walking in the Lake District would be even better.

So feeling slightly guilty about missing out on the 'Signs and Wonders' conference, I set off for Windermere with my tent and rucksack. The first night of my trip was greeted with what a local described as the worst storm in the last ten years. My tent withstood the force eight winds in the first part of the night, but succumbed to several inches of flood-water at five o'clock in the morning. As I retreated to the toilet block on the campsite I decided that I was very definitely in the wrong place! An act of God? Or just the Lake District being normal? The storm confirmed what I already knew – I needed to meet with God in Harrogate, not commune with nature in the Lake District.

Somewhat sheepishly I retraced my steps to the station early the next morning and returned home to make a late booking for the 'Signs and Wonders' conference. I arrived on the second morning of the conference as a late-registering

delegate and was consigned to the overflow hall. Watching
what was happening on the video screen, I found it difficult
to share fully in the atmosphere of the event, but was able to
see clearly what was happening. It's always difficult joining
a conference part way through, and though I had only missed
one session, it was obvious that a lot had happened which
needed explanation.

The session began with worship, and I was impressed by
the depth of love and intimacy which pervaded the singing
and the prayers. The music was all new to me and so I found
myself sitting back a little, sensing the atmosphere rather
than rushing to join in. This was a strange experience to
someone used to high-volume Methodist singing, but it felt
right. There was a sense of the presence and the peace of
God. The influence of 'Vineyard-style' worship has spread so
quickly that less than ten years later it seems strange that the
worship should have made such an impact, but it did. The
leaders stressed that worship was an intimate activity – yet
the sense of intimacy heightened rather than reduced the
sense of awe in the presence of God.

The teaching style was very Californian! Lots of humour,
very laid back and yet there was evidence of a tremendous
depth of biblical understanding. The sessions which had a
particular impact were those on the kingdom of God and on
worldview. The real shock came at the end of the session
when we moved into a clinic. There was no 'appeal', no
worship and no hype, just a time of waiting for the Holy
Spirit to move, and then a short stream of 'words of knowledge' which after some delay led to a number of people
coming forward for ministry. The conference delegates
seemed nervous about the delay, but John and his team
waited patiently for people to respond, appearing totally
confident that their words of knowledge were correct and
that God would move. When people came forward to receive
ministry, John explained how ministry would be done, then
instead of praying for people himself, asked members of his

team to pray while he kept up a running commentary – explaining the healing method, the manifestations of the Holy Spirit as they occurred and finished by interviewing some of the people who had received ministry. The ministry was both powerful and yet low-key in a way I had not experienced before.

As the conference went on I watched with interest as people were ministered to in much larger numbers than I had ever seen. The ministry was done by a team of Vineyard members who had accompanied John from America. John taught that ministering in the power of the Holy Spirit should be a normal Christian experience, that it did not depend upon maturity or upon a special gifting reserved for the chosen few, but solely upon the power of the Holy Spirit. At the beginning of one ministry session I approached one of the Vineyard pastors and asked if I could share in ministry with him. He readily agreed and afterwards took time to talk through all the things that had happened and answered some of my many questions.

So far I had been impressed by the quality of the worship, teaching and ministry, but I was still largely an observer. This changed dramatically on the last day! My roots are in the East Yorkshire farming community – a group not known for excessive demonstrations of emotion, and I am a person who has never found it easy to show my feelings except within a small group of trusted friends and family. However, God had a surprise (or was it a shock?) in store for me.

As the ministry time began at the end of the morning session, I was overwhelmed by a tremendous sense of the presence of God. I began to weep, noisily and uncontrollably. I was partially aware of what I was doing and embarrassed by it, and yet I was much more aware that what was happening was of God. Perhaps I could have stopped myself, I'm not sure – I certainly didn't want to stop. With hindsight I realise that God was releasing a lot of pain, frustration and dryness from me. I had been trying so hard to do God's will that I was worn out. I sobbed for a while, then I began to shake and sobbed a lot more. I'm not sure how long this experience lasted but I guess it was about half-an-hour.

At various points in this process, members of the Vineyard ministry team came and prayed with me. Two of them gave exactly the same prophecy with a gap of several minutes in between so they could not have known that they were saying the same thing. The prophecy was about breaking my heart of stone and giving me a shepherd's heart. They had no way of knowing that I was a minister, or that one-to-one pastoring is an aspect of my calling with which I have always struggled. Their words both increased my tears and released my pain. At the end of it, I felt both exhausted and at peace. It was as if a huge load had been lifted from me, a load that I only recognised as a problem when it had gone. The first of my problems – the need of a refreshing of my spiritual life – had definitely been met!

On my return to my home churches, I was both excited and apprehensive about sharing what had happened. When I did share it there was a mixed reaction. Some were intrigued and wanted to know more; others were extremely defensive and even hostile. Over the next year or so changes began to happen, but only very slowly. It seemed that some people were open and others were not. Strangely, casual contacts from outside the churches seemed almost more open than the Christians. This was despite the fact that the main catchment area for my two churches was a large council estate whose residents had very little interest in traditional Christianity. Attempts at outreach from the church had shown some fruit, but not nearly as much as I had hoped, and many of the people who showed an interest in Christianity only stayed with us for a very short time before drifting away.

A year later I looked forward to John's return to Britain – this time to Edinburgh. I booked into the conference together with my wife and my sister without any need for meteorological assistance. This time I was no longer surprised by the style of the conference and was much more able to concentrate on the teaching. I had also read *Power Evangelism* and *Power Healing* and had spent some time thinking about John's teaching.

In Edinburgh God again spoke very powerfully to me, this time through one of the ministry team. John McClure had been sharing about power evangelism, and as he had spoken I found myself becoming increasingly resentful. It seemed to me that his ministry was an unqualified success (he didn't actually say this) whereas so often my attempts at ministering in the power of the Spirit ended in failure. I have always struggled in the area of self-worth and can always see my failures more clearly than my successes. As the ministry time began I was not only resentful at the speaker, but also at God for placing me in such a difficult area. I sat in my seat mentally picturing the streets of North Hull and challenging God's ability to change the area where I lived. I wondered what would happen if John McClure came to Hull and tried to evangelise my neighbours. It all seemed terribly easy in America and almost impossible where I was. I was angry at God for putting me in such a difficult situation, and angry at myself for my inability to change things.

This resentful conversation with God had been going on for some time when I noticed that one of the ministry team was talking to my sister who was sitting with me. My sister turned to me and said that the lady from the ministry team had been told by God that I was a pastor and that she had a message from God for me, although it seemed nonsensical to her. I asked what the message was and she replied very simply, 'You can do it!' I remember very little of the ministry which followed, but that night I learnt a valuable lesson about trusting God. He does know what he is doing as he directs my life (and the lives of the congregation in my pastoral care) even when the evidence seems to point to the opposite.

Neither of these experiences led to an instant transformation of my personality, or of the churches in which I minister.

However, I have been aware of a gradual change, particularly in the way that I understand myself. Like many people, I have problems with self-worth, and still find it easier to believe criticism than praise. However, I am now much more certain that despite my inadequacies God can and does use me. I had known this in theory for years, but it's much harder to live it out. The power of God is contained in clay pots – I don't need to be perfect, God will use me as long as I am open.

Almost ten years later the church seems a very different place. I now lead a church in Oldham where ministry is a normal part of Sunday worship and there is a ministry team of twenty to thirty people all released to minister in prayer (using the five-step model from *Power Healing* (see p. 109), and large numbers of the congregation are happy to talk about the supernatural impact which the Holy Spirit has had upon their lives in salvation, healing, and equipping for ministry. I thank God for that storm in 1986. I'm glad that through John Wimber I was reintroduced to a deeper relationship with God and to his purpose for my ministry.

John Wimber and the Vineyard churches have been strongly associated with a new approach to worship and ministry – an approach stressing intimacy with God and the involvement of the whole body of Christ. It is not so often commented on but it is important to note that those churches have also been heavily involved in evangelism and church planting. It is no coincidence that churches like Holy Trinity Bromptom, St Andrew's, Chorleywood and St Thomas' Crookes in Sheffield have been pioneers in various forms of evangelism (especially the Alpha course) and in church planting. This emphasis has helped these churches to avoid becoming self-centred and introspective, which is a danger whenever one stresses healing and intimacy as vital elements in worship. It is too easy to fall into the trap of judging worship and indeed the whole life of the church on the basis of 'what's in it for me?'

In John Wimber's books and conferences he has rightly stressed the importance of the kingdom of God. This emphasis helps Christians to look outwards with a confidence that God's concern is for the whole of creation and that his purpose is that everyone should hear and receive the good news of Jesus Christ. This has come as a refreshing challenge to those of us who have assumed that only 10% of the population are likely to attend church and have adopted an almost fatalistic attitude to those who do not. The impact of John's teaching came at a providential moment for the church – poised for a Decade of Evangelism.

His stress on the sovereignty of the Holy Spirit to touch lives outside the church, and of a willingness by people who see church as irrelevant to allow the Holy Spirit to move in power in their lives, has acted as a powerful incentive for me and many others. We are encouraged to join God in working outside the walls of the church and to expect 'signs and wonders' in normal everyday situations. Since my conversion as a teenager I have longed for others to become Christians. The prophecy which confirmed my call to full-time ministry was that I would be used to go to people who do not know God and tell them of him. Because of this I have always been excited by movements of God's Holy Spirit which led to evangelism.

In the last decade or so there has been a tremendous upsurge of interest in reaching those who do not yet know Jesus Christ. John Wimber and the Vineyard Association is just one of many movements stressing this. Willow Creek, DAWN, Minus to Plus and various Decade of Evangelism initiatives have challenged the church to become more involved in evangelising the world. This is particularly important in view of the fact that the traditional denominations are continuing to lose members, especially younger members. If the movement of the Holy Spirit which began in the 'charismatic movement' in the 1960s and continued with the 'third wave' in the 1980s and the 'Toronto blessing' in the 1990s is to have a significant lasting effect on the world as we know it (and particularly here in England), then the impact of renewal on the church must be seen to spill out into the unchurched world to a far greater extent than we have seen so far.

Another important contribution John Wimber has made to the area of evangelism is in challenging the worldview which dominates so much of the thought process in America and Europe. This worldview assumes that we have moved from a religious understanding of the universe to a scientific one and that the two are incompatible. Science has disproved religion! This is not true, but is accepted by many people, including a lot of Christians. This has made the church very hesitant in evangelism. We don't expect people to believe what we do and are, therefore, reluctant to share our faith.

It has been my experience that the renewal of the Holy Spirit has led to an increase in confidence in two areas which are vital in evangelism. The first area is that of assurance. Because I am confident of my place in God's family, I am much more confident about inviting others to join. This assurance is partly a result of the infilling presence of the Holy Spirit, and is partly a result of personal commitment born out of good teaching.

The second area is that of faith that others will believe. In the nineteenth century the Primitive Methodists placed a great emphasis on 'getting into faith'; that is, in praying through a situation until they had faith that a church could be planted, that it was God's will that it should be planted, and furthermore that no power on earth or in heaven could prevent it from being planted. I believe that this sort of faith is gradually being rediscovered in the traditional denominations today. If this is the case, then the growth of the church and the increased presence of the kingdom of God in the world around us will become more and more pronounced. There are a large number of men and women of God who have played important parts in this rediscovery of the power of God – and I am sure that John Wimber is one of them.

CHAPTER TWELVE

John Leach

John Leach (b. 1952) was ordained into the Anglican minis-
try in 1981. He served his first curacy at St Nicholas', North
Walsham in Norfolk, and then spent four years on the staff of
St Thomas' Crookes, Sheffield. He is now vicar of St James'
Styvechale in Coventry. As a liturgist and musician he is a
member of GROW (The Group for Renewal of Worship) and
the PRAXIS council. Among his publications is Liturgy and
Liberty *(MARC 1989).*

'Love the message, love the miracles, *love* the man, hate the
music!'

This was my reaction to my first Wimber conference, at
Westminster Central Hall in 1984. As a seasoned Spring
Harvester whose musical tastes tended more in the direction
of reggae and heavy metal than 'west coast' soft rock I found
Vineyard music something of a culture shock. It did nothing
for me, I'm afraid, particularly in forty-five-minute doses,
and I was sure it wouldn't catch on over here.

But as we engaged in ever longer times of worship, I began
to see things happening which surprised me. As they got used
to it, I could see people becoming increasingly rapt in worship. Once John had taught us to recognise it, I could see the

Spirit's presence on people as they worshipped. One friend told me later that the worship at the conference had taken him to places with Jesus he'd never ever been to before. And within a few short years Britain was every bit as familiar with Vineyard songs as with anything home-produced. Now a decade and more later it has become a major force in British renewal worship, and has evolved itself along the way. Whatever one made of it personally, there was clearly a powerful anointing of God on the music of John and his colleagues.

So what are its distinctives, and how have they touched the British scene?

First of all, it is worth noting that in Vineyardspeak 'worship' equals 'music'. Whilst quite liturgical in their own way, Vineyard services deliberately give no place whatsoever to what Anglicans, Romans or Methodists would call 'liturgy'. John's impact on the worship scene is largely a musical impact, but nonetheless impressive for that.

Having said that, of course, it isn't quite that simple. John places great importance on cultivating a lifestyle of worship, so that what happens in church on a Sunday is only a continuation of what happens in our hearts and at other meetings of Christians together during the week. That each worshipper should have a 'secret life with God' is vitally important to the worshipping life of the church as it gathers. But it is music which is central, a belief which sprang not from dogma but from empirical observation of the church at worship.

The musical style originated, as you might expect, from the California soft rock scene, and back in 1984 it was not dissimilar to the sort of thing that Wimber's group, The Righteous Brothers, might have performed a couple of decades earlier. The lyrics were unashamedly intimate and loving, and songs were sung *to* Jesus, and hardly ever simply *about* him. It was totally lyric-based, and there was no space at all for instrumental passages or displays of musical virtuosity, although I remember John himself sitting in with the band and adding some quite exquisite piano parts to the mainly guitar-based songs. Melodically and harmonically there was nothing special going on; simplicity was the name of the game. As far as I can remember the 1984 repertoire consisted of only one song already known to British worshippers (and they did that with the wrong chords), so we were in for a pretty steep learning curve during the conference.

The style of the songs was deliberately simple so that worship in small groups during the week could use the same material without the resources of the full band used on Sundays. During a visit to an Anaheim kinship group in 1986 I found that the same songs, played by one not very good guitarist, could have the same effect on people as they were led into God's presence. The repertoire was small, and the intention, at least in the early days, was that songs could quickly be learnt by heart, so that the distractions of songsheets or OHPs would be eliminated. As the music has grown and evolved songs have increased in number and complexity, but the emphasis is still on heart-to-heart worship with as little as possible to get in the way.

It wasn't just the songs which were different back in the eighties, though. The whole style of worship leading was new. At our churches we might have heard, 'Now we'll sing number 274 . . . Now has anyone got a favourite?'; at Spring Harvest we were encouraged with voice-overs between the songs which on a good day didn't quite turn into fully-fledged sermons; now all we got was a mumbled 'Number 7' and off we went. It was all very sink-or-swim; you certainly didn't get wound up or manipulated by, or receive any help from (depending on your point of view) Carl Tuttle or the other worship leaders of those halcyon days. It seemed clearly to be a case of 'He must increase, I must decrease', and the music went on and either took you along with it or left you high and dry as the leader faded from view to be replaced by Jesus himself.

Actually, much of the British renewal scene did get taken along, and the impact of this whole new style of worship can't be underestimated in looking at the worshipping church today. In trying to analyse that impact, I want to talk about four rich gifts we've received from John, and three ways they've affected us.

Firstly, John has reminded us about the absolute centrality of worship. We're not here primarily to preach the gospel, to fight for social justice, or even to heal the sick, vital though these things are to the life of the church. First and foremost we're here to glorify God, and everything else we do must spring not just from times of worship but from lives of worship. Without this emphasis I've seen those passionate about the gospel become hard-edged and legalistic, and those passionate about social concern become angry and embittered. To focus on God first, and let our other passions become secondary to passion about Jesus, prevents us from falling into either of these traps.

This shows itself practically in the amount of time given to worship in Vineyard events, and the place it has on just about every agenda. I often wonder how my own Church Council meetings would go if we began with forty-five minutes of singing!

Secondly, in formulating his philosophy of worship, John knew exactly what he was doing. Whether or not you liked it personally, there was no denying that Vineyard worship had, and has, a set of clearly thought-out principles behind it. It was only later that I read anything John had written on the subject, but it was clear that the look of Vineyard worship on the outside represented a definite underlying philosophy. As with most of what John did, there was always a reason, a clearly-articulated vision and set of values, and a desire to be rigorously scriptural. We have so much to learn in the church about this, particularly in worship. When I'm in a church (other than my own, of course!) and the minister or worship leader tells us that we're going to sing such-and-such a song or hymn, I often want to shout out 'Why?' Vast amounts of what we do in church life seems to be done . . . well, just because that's how we do it. It's not surprising, therefore, that so much of it seems purposeless: John and his worship teach us to let what people see us doing speak of the deeper reasons for doing it. I'm sure that it wouldn't be right for all of us to worship with John's philosophy and values, but we do need to worship with *ours*. However different they may be from those of the Vineyard, we nevertheless need to have them, and to let them drive all we do.

Thirdly, John knew where he was going. Vineyard worship is worship with a purpose. Its twin goals are intimacy with Jesus and the exaltation of his name: nothing more, nothing less. The style tells us that this takes time, and that we can so easily be distracted along the way, even by well-meaning worship leaders. I could imagine myself as a worshipper lying on a lilo drifting gently out to sea under the warm sun, with the land and all its human distractions getting further and further away and intruding less and less on my reverie. The music laps gently around me, with never an unexpected toss to its waves to startle or surprise me. Eventually it's just me, the sun and the ripples.

It's not that the Vineyard didn't know how to celebrate exuberantly with up-tempo songs: there was *Hosanna*, and of course . . . well, *Hosanna*. But that type of song was clearly the prelude to the real thing: quiet intimacy.

The goal of this intimacy is to experience the presence of God. As the singing comes to an end there is a time of silence, pregnant with the Spirit's hovering over the congregation. This is the time when spiritual gifts may be exercised. There may be a prophetic word for the congregation, or an impassioned prayer of intercession. Individuals may feel the touch of God on them, and there may be spontaneous healings or deliverance. Or the congregation as a whole may be overcome with weeping or laughing. People's hearts are softened to receive the teaching which is to follow, although on a really good day God may take over completely and the sermon may be dispensed with. I remember one occasion when, after several false starts, John shut his notes, waited, made an appeal, and watched about 300 people come forward to dedicate or rededicate their lives to Christ. Intimacy with God pure and simple is the goal, but when that intimacy is reached, things happen.

Whilst I'm not sure this is the only valid way of understanding worship, it clearly is an important way. The modern church music of the sixties was packed full of right-on social concern, (the lyrics of songs in *Youth Praise*, especially Volume Two, provide a fascinating commentary on the issues of the era), and seventies renewal music was often dominated by happy-clappy ditties which I suppose we needed to provide a more exciting alternative to the trad hymns and chanted psalms which had been pretty much our sole diet. But it took John to remind the British church about real and deep intimacy with Jesus, not just in worship but throughout their lives. It's not that they don't care about social issues in Southern California. On the contrary, the Vineyard has done pioneering work and has much to teach us on that subject. It's not that they don't know how to celebrate at times, it's just that worship is a serious business and Jesus, not ourselves or the world around, must be central. Whatever we may think of the idea, I'm sure Jesus is thrilled to bits that his bride has learnt to spend time in quiet closeness to him: John's part in the learning of that lesson seems to me to be paramount.

If John wanted to lead the church to this place of intimacy with her Lord he knew, fourthly, how to get her there. With that destination in view, Vineyard worship plots out very clearly the path for us to walk along during the journey. The seamlessness of the music, the Christocentricity of the lyrics and the unobtrusive leading all conspire to keep Jesus at the very centre of our attention. The length of time taken for the journey, while it may exhaust those with less spiritual stamina, provides time for even the slowest to get there and enjoy God's presence if they want to.

This, too, challenges much British worship praxis. With our Nonconformist hymn sandwiches or our Anglican or Roman liturgy sandwiches we rarely do *anything* for long enough to allow the time it takes for us to meet with God, let alone to spend time in his presence lost in wonder, love and praise. Vineyard worship reminds a busy church that intimacy can only be found at a cost: marriages can founder through lack of quality time, and so, sadly, can the relationship between Christ and his bride. John has taught us how to give that time to God in worship.

Things have moved on from those early days. As with the Vineyard movement itself, there has been an evolution and enriching, as that which was born out of the creativity of one man began to be transferred to others. John's philosophy of 'equipping the saints', whilst holding firm to key values, has led to an enriching of the worship model without its ever losing those original emphases. Younger men have brought their gifts as musicians, and to some extent things have moved with the times. There has been a recognition of the power music has of itself, even without words, to express worship and to move the hearts of worshippers (I remember an unidentified American Vineyard band playing at St Andrew's, Chorleywood, with a brilliant soprano sax player who was so smoky it made your hair curl). People like Kevin Prosch have explored the world of 'Prophetic Worship', although as you might imagine in some different ways from British musicians going the same way. And above all a mightily successful marketing policy of audio tapes and CDs has shown the arranging and production gifts of Vineyard musicians, and flooded the British Isles with hundreds of tracks of the highest quality.

Now there are British soundalike bands. As Vineyard churches began to be planted this side of the Atlantic, and established churches bought into Vineyard styles and values, native worship leaders and musicians began to distribute their wares alongside the originals. And the latest wave of the Spirit from Toronto Airport ex-Vineyard has brought a whole new set of emphases, with a much more celebratory style, a greater understanding of the power of instrumental music and the creative arts in general, and lots of songs about rivers and rain.

So how has the British church responded? Of course there have been parodies. Carl Tuttle's mid-80s semi-narcoleptic 'Number seven' in D major is so wonderfully imitable, and songs 'in the style of' have apparently included the classic *Lord I just want to praise you for your awesomeness* and the marginally irreverent *Lord you are much sweeter than rhubarb*! But we only imitate what we value, and it seems to me that the contribution of John and the Vineyard to the British worshipping scene has been immense and important. I believe that there are three main ways in which we have benefited from his style and philosophy of worship.

Some churches, firstly, have bought the lot – lock, stock and barrel – the songs, the style, the theology behind it: all of which seem to make such good sense, and to deliver the goods in practice. So they have just done it. Anglican services can begin with up to thirty minutes of laid-back singing, one song following the last uninterrupted by anything remotely liturgical. Or New Churches can follow the Vineyard framework of worship, word and ministry completely. Many of the large, famous charismatic churches of Britain, and particularly Anglican ones, seem to have found a style which feels exactly right for them, and judging by their growth, for others too.

Intimacy with Jesus is firmly back on the agenda, and from this worship style flows a ministry style which also looks distinctively Wimberish. My impression (without having actually counted) is that charismatic Anglican churches have been those most readily accepting of the Vineyard ethos. I suspect it resonates with the gentle dignity which is the stuff of traditional Anglicanism. I can imagine a really keen Pentecostal being slightly bored by the whole thing. But there are now plenty of British churches which look similar to a good Californian Vineyard at worship, and many of them are growing significantly.

Secondly, there are those churches which, in good post-modern fashion, pick-and-mix their worship repertoire and style. They don't buy the Vineyard philosophy completely. They may feel that whilst keeping our eyes on Jesus is a good thing to do, we mustn't get tunnel vision and forget that there are other aspects to worship. A different strand (although one which is as far as I know on exceptionally good terms with John) is that of the Make Way/March for Jesus school. Still rather Jesus-centred, I would say, but managing to move wider than just me and him gazing into each other's eyes, and into the realms of intercession and spiritual warfare, remembering perhaps that for every person who can reach intimacy with Jesus there are over twenty in Britain who can't or won't. Having said that, there are some good songs issuing from the Vineyard, so let's use them, and let's use them particularly for those moments when it is right simply to spend time with the Lord one-to-one. If there was a gap in this area of the market, it has been beautifully and success-fully filled by the Vineyard.

And not just the renewal market either. The simplicity and beauty of the songs has given some of them much wider appeal. It is not uncommon to hear robed church choirs singing Vineyard songs in carefully arranged four-part har-mony, probably to the delight of worthy Anglican ladies who would have a fit if their church suddenly bought the rest of the package!

Thus whether you agree completely or even partially with John's philosophy behind his worship, the material itself is fair game to be culled and lumped into a repertoire along with anything else you fancy. Many churches would find huge holes in their worship if all the Vineyard songs were suddenly removed. Thus it is a paradox that some churches, which would run a mile from the things John has taught about ministry in the power of the Spirit, are nevertheless meeting God through his music. I wonder if that saddens him or gladdens his heart?

Thirdly, there must be areas where the opposite is true. We agree with the theology; we too are after deep intimacy with Jesus; we too know that it takes time, and we're prepared to set apart that time: we just don't like that type of music. Even in churches which for purely stylistic reasons reject the music, the philosophy behind it still speaks, and again John has influenced those who would look as if they had rejected him. As the British scene branched out more and more into different styles of music, as staid English congregations sway to reggae or bop to Latin beats, they do it for the good old reasons; to exalt the name of Jesus and to meet him face to face. The lessons John has taught about our relationship with God, the possibility of his meeting with us powerfully and at times dramatically, and the relentless pursuit of evangelism, church growth and social concern have been well learnt, but we'd just rather do it to a different tune, a bit less like Radio 2.

So whichever option you plump for, it is indisputable that John has influenced the British renewal scene and its worship in some highly significant ways. It is right to give profound thanks to God for him, and although my purpose is to write simply about his worship, I do need to sneak in a personal tribute to a man whose effect on my personal ministry has been second to none, in all sorts of areas. It's not just that he says the right things: he says them so graciously and in a way so oozing with the love of God. Even those who oppose most of what John stands for recognise in him a humility and love, a desire to bless the body of Christ around the world, and a grace which is truly Christlike. He wouldn't like my saying that, of course. I remember an angry response at one conference when we tried to applaud him. 'There are no heroes in the body of Christ,' he snapped, and we all felt suitably rebuked. So maybe instead I should give the glory to Jesus for sending the church such a significant man with such an important ministry, not least in the area of worship.

So what about me and the music? After all these years, has my view of Vineyard worship changed since 1984? Well, if you're ever passing, pop into St James' and hear our version of *I Give You All The Honour* Bob Marley style!

CHAPTER THIRTEEN

Chris Lane

After an early start in business, Chris Lane *became a lay industrial chaplain in Leeds before being ordained in the Church of England. Following a curacy in Holbeck, Leeds, Chris joined the staff of St Andrew's, Chorleywood, as assistant to Bishop David Pytches, in his capacity as UK Director of Vineyard Ministries International. Then after a year as an intern pastor at the Anaheim Vineyard, Southern California, Chris and his family returned to England in 1987 to found the St Albans Vineyard Christian Fellowship. Chris and his wife Fliss have been involved in several ' church plants' and now have pastoral oversight of Vineyard churches in the Midlands.*

Wimber lent forward and said, 'Chris . . . you don't know the first thing about church-planting. In fact you don't even know the right questions to ask!' My heart sank and I sat there exhausted and embarrassed. We were having lunch in a small Italian restaurant in Yorba Linda, California. The sun shone through the small pane windows and highlighted the dust suspended in the air. 'Well that's it!' I thought. 'Dust, dust and more dust. My whole life's turning to dust. What do we do now?'

Ten years previously I'd have known exactly what to do. Life was so much simpler then. You would have found us busily expanding our jewellery business in Harrogate, North Yorkshire. We were young and 'successful' and starting a family. Then God began to move in on our lives and things started getting complicated. Two years later, we were selling up and reluctantly pursuing a call to the ministry, much to the amazement of ourselves, our friends and our family. I say 'reluctantly' because we had fallen head over heels in love with Jesus but with no church background, neither of us could make head or tail of the church. We kept asking ourselves the question, 'How could Jesus be so wonderful, his word so compelling and his church so out of touch with people like us?'

We were still in this state of consternation when I began my first curacy in an inner-city parish in Leeds. By now, a number of friends and most of our family had become Christians. All of us from unchurched backgrounds. My father-in-law, a successful businessman and new convert, struggled more than most to make sense of the church. Unfortunately, I was defensive and perceived tensions between him and myself, because I believed that he thought that I had sold out and was now a part of 'the establishment'. So when he came to me, 'hot foot' from St Michael-le-Belfry's in York, enthusing about an American preacher called John Wimber, I was in no mood to hear him. However, when he offered me an all-expenses-paid trip to London, including a nice hotel, just so I could attend Wimber's first Westminster Conference, I thought to myself 'Well I may be stupid but I'm not that stupid! You're on!'

Wimber walked onto the stage and sat down behind the piano. 'What am I doing here?' I thought. 'This is just what we need . . . another fat American telling us what to do!' Carl Tuttle struck up the first song. I got to my feet and fumbled around for the songsheet. After a while I gave up and just listened. The worship was different. It wasn't traditional. It wasn't 'happy clappy'. It was just different. I puzzled for a moment or two. There was something familiar about it . . . Then it struck me. It was contemporary music – very 'west coast' American – not too far from the sort of thing I listened to at home. I was pleasantly surprised. I made another effort to find my songsheet and follow the words. They turned out to be very direct and personal. The first song finished and the next started up . . . same formula.

The next thirty or forty minutes turned out to be something of a revelation. Here was a way in which I could worship the Jesus I knew and loved without going through some kind of cultural airlock. I was excited by the style of music. Then something happened and the words began to get to me. 'Hold me Lord, in your arms . . .' went the song. Tears began to well up and threatened to embarrass me. I felt the Lord's presence on me. 'Not now Lord! . . . Not here Lord!' I protested. 'I know people here and besides my father-in-law might see me!' Then a familiar but forgotten voice said: 'This is the way, walk in it.' Waves of relief rolled over me. I didn't care too much after that. I'd found a home.

For the rest of the week, I thought I'd died and gone to heaven. It was the worship that did it. God had put a song in my heart, and John Wimber and the Vineyard showed me how to sing it. First and foremost I'm grateful for that. But that wasn't all. After several years as a charismatic Christian, I had more questions than answers, and my cynicism was the fruit of some pretty heavy-duty disillusionment. As John taught us about the kingdom of God, pieces started to fall into place. It was very like working on a large jigsaw. I'd spent years in private study and theological education and all I had to show for it were pieces that still bore little or no relationship to the 'big picture'. Suddenly, things started to fit together. It was really very exciting. And then there were the 'clinics'.

The ministry times, or 'clinics' as they were called, amazed me. I well remember the first time Wimber introduced a clinic. I'd thoroughly enjoyed the worship and had chuckled through his testimony. I was warming to the man. And then he prepared to commit professional suicide before my very eyes. I was appalled. I felt compassion and concern for him as a fellow human being. I wanted him to stop. Why doesn't somebody say something? I thought. We've all had a wonderful evening. Let's just go home now and we'll come back tomorrow. But John, with characteristic grace, humility and courage, pressed on. 'Come Holy Spirit!' he prayed.

During the course of the next hour I witnessed more power than I'd experienced in the whole previous seven years of charismatic Christianity. And so it went on throughout the week. Blind eyes saw, legs grew, demons were cast out and Jesus was preached to the poor as the ministry team swarmed through the London Underground chewing gum and praying for anything that moved! A conference that started with two thousand delegates rapidly grew to over five thousand as 'overflow' meetings overflowed into more 'overflow' meetings. The pavement outside was cluttered with wheelchairs and the like and many received prayer and ministry as they queued on the street. John himself prayed for relatively few people, preferring to train and release others to minister. By the end of the week we were all doing it. It was wonderful. And again I shall always be grateful to John for showing me what can happen when you let Jesus have *his* church back, and equip the saints for the work of the ministry (Eph 4:11,12).

In the aftermath of the Westminster conference, I went back to Leeds full of fresh vision and vigour. The following year my wife, Fliss, went to the Wimber conference in Sheffield and had an equally significant time. Our ministry in Leeds flourished, under the wise and watchful eye of John Holmes, the vicar of St Luke's, Holbeck. But our time there was coming to an end, and although we dearly would have loved to stay, this was not possible. Once again we found ourselves asking some fundamental questions about models of church as we knew them, and in spite of the wonderful refreshment we had received from God, we were still haunted by those early memories and questions: 'How could Jesus be so wonderful, his word so compelling and his church so out of touch with people like us?'

It was as we were considering this question that I had a deeply unsettling dream. In it I was crossing a huge and expansive plain on a well made-up road. At some distance and straddling the road was a very large and substantial building. I knew it to be my destination and the road led straight to the door. However, as I approached the building I became disconcerted because everything seemed very quiet and still. I approached the large and imposing door and when I tried the handles, the doors swung inward. It was then I realised with a start that my supposed destination was a façade, and that the road I was on continued unbroken beneath the door and across the plain into a dim and uncertain future. As I said, the dream was very unsettling, but it triggered in Fliss and myself a discussion about 'doing a church plant for people like us' – whatever that meant! But that was before God made us an offer we could not refuse.

At the Westminster conference John Wimber had referred me to Bishop David Pytches who had kindly prayed for me. David told me afterwards that he was intending to run some occasional days for leaders and would I be interested? I said I would and duly asked to be put on the mailing list. A year later Fliss and I finally made the trek from Leeds down to Chorleywood and at the end of a very helpful and encouraging day we shook hands with David and thanked him for his hospitality. As it happened we were the last ones out and stood there chatting for some five or ten minutes. A few months later, out of the blue, David rang us and asked us whether we would like to come down to Chorleywood to discuss a job. We were absolutely flabbergasted but very excited. The job sported the grandiose title of 'Assistant to

Bishop David Pytches, UK Director of Vineyard Ministries International'. Needless to say we jumped at it!

Our two years at St Andrew's, Chorleywood were rich and exciting, but within six weeks of our arrival we knew that we had not 'arrived' and would be moving on. David suggested that we attended a Vineyard pastors' conference at Anaheim in Southern California. We went expecting a charismatic 'knees up', but were disappointed to discover that we had enrolled ourselves on a church growth and leadership conference.

However, Wimber was on form and in his element. Having been a church growth consultant for a number of years, he had personal experience of hundreds of churches. He had met and 'dialogued' with thousands of pastors. It dawned on us that Wimber was so much more than 'Mr Signs and Wonders' as the British press had taken to calling him. Unlike the Westminster conference, where we had been able to draw on past study and experience; church growth and leadership were wholly new territory for us and came as something of a shock. The week turned out to be a rich but rather indigestible feast. We came away with more questions than answers, most of them relating to the way we were going about things back home. But perhaps more fundamentally, we finally realised as a result of meeting pastors from all over the world there were as many different ways of 'doing church' as there was sand on the seashore, and depending on what you were trying to do, some of them worked better than others.

When we got back to Chorleywood, we knew that even at St Andrew's, we had not found the answer to our fundamental question: 'How could Jesus be so wonderful, his word so compelling and his church so out of touch with people like us?' Whilst greatly appreciating the Spirit-led vitality and flavour of St Andrew's, we knew that there had to be room for many more variations on that same Spirit-led vitality if we were going to 'reach the nation'. Of course, all this sounds quite obvious now, but to us at that time it was very radical.

So we talked and prayed and prayed and talked, and we got to the point where we knew we couldn't just keep *talking* about it, we were going to have to *do* something. In Bishop David Pytches we had a wonderful mentor. We were able to bounce our ideas off him as one, who through his experiences in South America, was used to innovation and experiment in mission. We began to explore with him the concept of 'church planting'. He had reservations about institutional practicalities in the English situation but was generally encouraging.

It was decided that we would go to the Diocesan Bishop, John Taylor, and offer our services as church planters. When we eventually met with his assistant, we explained that we were willing to fund and support ourselves in exchange for the freedom to try an experiment in church planting and if we were successful to train others to do the same. Yes, it would need careful and sensitive handling because of the Church of England's parish system, but we were confident that there was a way forward and that things could be worked out. Two or three weeks later we received a letter from the Bishop which left us stunned.

In the letter the Bishop said that he would not be willing to support a church planting initiative such as ours. Furthermore, he had consulted the diocesan lawyers and, if we were to pursue this, we would be regarded as 'schismatics' and our only appropriate action was to resign from holy orders. The letter left us in a state of shock. We kept asking ourselves 'Have we really got this so wrong?' However, when David Pytches saw the letter he was flabbergasted and strongly protested on our behalf. Fliss and I then became concerned that St Andrew's would be drawn into an unhelpful confrontation. This was *our* thing and *our* responsibility. It had never been a St Andrew's project, ploy or plot, and the last thing we wanted was to create tensions between St Andrew's and the diocese.

In the event we decided to go quietly. When the dust had settled we came to the realisation that we were caught 'between a rock and a hard place'. Insofar as we knew Jesus we believed that he had called us to be church planters, and we were to go and do that even if it meant dying in the attempt. We could not stay but we could not go – at least not as Anglicans. So whilst trying to put a brave face on it, we decided to resign from the staff at St Andrew's, and start working independently somewhere. We felt about as much enthusiasm for this as a condemned man eating his final breakfast. Then one night the phone rang. It was John Mumford who, with his wife Ele, was doing an internship at the Anaheim Vineyard Church in Southern California.

'So you're going then?' said John.

'Well yes . . . we don't know what else we can do,' I said wearily. 'It seems as if the Lord's got us over a barrel on this one. We can't deny that he's spoken so we have no choice but to go.'

'Hmm . . . ,' said John, 'Wimber's been following this one very closely. He was concerned that it might get out of hand and damage St Andrew's and hence the renewal, but now he wants to know if you would like to come over and see him. He says he'll pay.'

'What? That's incredible! I hardly know what to say!' I blurted. 'John *please* will you thank him for his concern . . . but as far as coming over . . . of course we'd love to but . . . I'm sorry John we have a problem.'

'What's that?' said John.

'Well,' I said hesitantly, 'I'd need to bring the whole family.'

'What! How many of you are there?' John asked incredulously.

'Six,' I said sheepishly.

'Six! Why do you need to bring the whole family?'

'Well we're all in this together John, and it's going to be a big sacrifice for the kids too,' I explained. 'So we promised them that the next time we went to the States we'd all go so they could see for themselves the sort of thing we were trying to build together. We've been trying to save up to come . . . I'm sorry . . . It's very embarrassing.'

'Well I'll ask Chris, but don't raise your hopes.'

True to his word Mumford explained the situation to Wimber, and three weeks later we were all on a plane to California.

And so it was that in a conversation a day or so later Wimber said, 'Chris, you don't know the first thing about church planting.' The waiter took our dishes away and returned with the dessert menu, but my appetite had gone. Of course Wimber was right, we didn't know a thing about church planting, and it stung to think that we weren't even asking the right questions.

'Well thank God for his honesty,' I thought. 'But what do we do now Lord?'

'However,' Wimber continued, 'I've been following you guys. You've handled yourselves well. What's more, I believe God's put a call on you, and if you want to become a Vineyard pastor, we'll bring the whole family over to California again, and we'll train you, give you everything we've got, and then see where we go from there. How does that sound?'

John's eyes were twinkling. For a moment or two I was dumb-struck. I couldn't believe what I was hearing. Then for the second time in a Wimber meeting, waves of relief rolled over me. I didn't know whether to laugh or to cry. A voice somewhere said, 'This is the way, walk in it.' I don't know what moved me the most, John's love, generosity or quite simply that he believed in us.

'Well? What do you think?'

'John,' I said breathlessly, 'I hardly know what to say, except that I think God just rescued us. But won't this mean that you get a lot of criticism or something?'

John shook his head and laughed. 'Don't you worry about that. I live in a swirl of criticism!'

'Well. Thank you. I still don't know what to say. We'll need to talk to the kids though before we can give you an answer.'

'Sure!' he beamed. 'Hey! How about some dessert now!!'

When we finally moved over to Anaheim we criss-crossed with John and Ele Mumford who were returning to start the first Vineyard in south west London. Our year in Anaheim was a fascinating experience. As well as routine pastoral duties, we and another couple, Rick and Lulu Williams, had weekly church planting tutorials with Todd Hunter. Todd had been responsible for pioneering umpteen Vineyard churches in West Virginia. He was quite simply the best the Vineyard had at that time. In addition to this, we looked forward to regular sessions with Wimber, where we fired what we hoped were the 'right' questions at him in rapid succession!

John's generosity in terms of time, energy and money still takes my breath away. When the time came for us to leave, we all bore what had become a heavy sense of responsibility.

'I don't know how we're going to pay you back John,' I said forlornly. 'You've invested so much in us and yet at the end of the day, we still don't know if it's going to work!'

With typical generosity Wimber replied, 'Hey, you don't owe us a thing! We're just trying to give away what God gave us. You just go and do the same.'

When we returned to England, the Williams went to Teddington, and we went to St Albans in Hertfordshire, which stands at the intersection of the M1 and M25 motorways. We arrived with a few thousand pounds in savings and a bit of furniture. Fortunately, we knew another couple whom we had met just before we went to the States and were also living in St Albans. And what's more they were worship leaders so you could say we had a head start!

The next two years were terrible. Fliss went to work at a local playgroup, and I started a painting and decorating business in order to try to keep our heads above water. There was everything to do and no time to do it. In addition, one of our children contracted meningitis while on holiday and nearly died. We frequently felt very lonely and desperate. There were times when I would writhe in an agony of fear and desperation crying out to God. However, throughout this time, Wimber kept in touch with us all. He sent Todd Hunter over to see us. He paid for us to go over to Denver to attend a Pastors' conference. And every time he came over to England, there was an invitation to meet him somewhere for a meal. God bless him. Like our heavenly Father, he was always mindful of us and never abandoned us.

During this time the church slowly and steadily began to grow. Ironically, our first convert left us to join St Albans Abbey, which was a bit of a blow and set us thinking! We majored on the things John had taught us. Telling the story of Jesus, telling our story, worship, training and equipping, evangelism and gathering, ministering to the poor, developing small groups and building infrastructure, etc, and always prayer, always more prayer. It was as exhausting as it sounds.

Eight years on we have to say that God has been faithful and blessed us. St Albans Vineyard continues to grow slowly and steadily, currently running at about three hundred people with a number of full and part time staff. In addition, we've planted churches in Hull, Southampton and Darmstadt, Germany. As a movement, we are organised into regions with 'co-ordinators' overseeing the pastoral care and mission in their areas. We've held on to our vision, and concentrated on developing church planters and leaders, rather than adopting other churches. March 1996 marked a milestone in the development of the Association of Vineyard Churches in this country when Wimber laid hands on John and Ele Mumford, passing on to them his oversight of us all and establishing us as an autonomous wing of the worldwide

Vineyard movement. Not only have we come home, but by the grace of God we've come of age.

Would all of this have happened without Wimber? Who knows with a God who can cause the very stones to call out and praise him? But I think not. If John and Carol Wimber taught us anything at all it was this. God loves his church, and just as we believe in God so he believes in us, choosing to work with us rather than without us.

Of course that kind of faith is risky. The Wimbers' chose to believe in us and said, 'Come on let's try this thing together. Watch how we do it. Now you try.' Thanks John. Thanks Carol.

But above all, thank God!

CHAPTER FOURTEEN

Martin Robinson

The Rev Dr Martin Robinson is Director for Mission and Theology at the Bible Society and a minister of the Churches of Christ in Birmingham. He is a well-established conference speaker and writer who in his spare time enjoys jogging, travelling and exploring other cultures. His most recent books include Planting Tomorrow's Churches Today *(Monarch, 1992),* The Faith of the Unbeliever *(Monarch, 1994), and* To Win the West *(Monarch, 1996).*

It is almost impossible to assess the contribution of any leader without also commenting on the significance and place of the movement which they lead. John Gunstone writes of the 'Wimber-Vineyard ministry'[1] and I am sure that he is correct to do so. The movement and the man belong together.

Both Vineyard and Wimber are part of that broader twentieth century phenomenon – the Pentecostal movement. Wimber gladly acknowledges his debt to the Pentecostals but at the same time claims that Vineyard is a new 'wave' within that movement. How justified is such a claim and what does it really mean?

In all probability, it was Peter Wagner who first coined the term 'third wave' to describe the stream of Christianity represented by Wimber and Vineyard. He used it to distinguish Wimber from the first wave of Pentecostals, sometimes called the 'classical Pentecostals' who have formed their own Pentecostal denominations, and the second wave of Pentecostals, usually called 'charismatics' who have received a pentecostal experience but remained in their historic denominations.

In using such a term – 'the third wave' – Wagner is drawing on a much older Pentecostal tradition. Frank Bartleman, amongst others, had described the first Pentecostal outbreak as another wave of revival breaking in on God's church. The early Pentecostals were well aware that they were part of an older holiness tradition stretching back to Wesley and others. The classical Pentecostals drew heavily on the spirituality and theology of the holiness movement for their self-understanding and expression.

The charismatics, located as they were in the historic churches, certainly did not feel themselves to be part of a holiness tradition and were only too glad to shed the earlier description of themselves as 'neo-Pentecostals' for a term that introduced some distance between themselves and the older Pentecostal denominations. Charismatics acknowledged that they were part of the same movement – 'Pentecost outside of Pentecost',[2] but claimed that although they had inherited a Pentecostal theology at the outset, they were now developing a different, and by implication, more sophisticated, theology. Some writers described the charismatic phase of Pentecostalism as the 'second wind' of the Spirit.

The puzzled observer might wonder why Wimber sees himself as something other than part of the charismatic movement. Why the need for a 'third wave' as compared with a 'second wind'? Wimber's spiritual journey seemed to follow an almost classical pattern of involvement in the charismatic movement. The only significant difference seems to be that his involvement in charismatic experiences came relatively late on in the development of that movement in California.

Wimber's early explanation for the difference seems curious to a British eye. Quoting Wagner, who he appears to endorse, he claims that:

'The third wave began around 1980 with the opening of an increasing number of traditional evangelical churches and institutions to the supernatural working of the Holy Spirit, even though they were not, nor did they wish to become, either Pentecostal or charismatic.'[3]

Wagner's and Wimber's claim that it was the context rather than any difference in the content of the message seems strange to British ears simply because the introduction of Wimber to a British audience came about almost entirely through Anglican leaders and churches which were strongly associated with the charismatic movement in Britain. The three most prominent churches, Holy Trinity, Brompton; St Michael-le-Belfry in York; and St Andrew's, Chorleywood, were all seen as leading shapers of the charismatic movement in England if not in the British Isles as a whole.

But the time element was in reality a very significant factor. By the time of Wimber's arrival in Britain, the charismatic movement was suffering from a lack of direction. The early hope of the charismatic pioneers that the movement would renew and equip the church for both growth and unity had proved unfounded. By the mid-1980s many of the early leaders were not as prominent as they had once been. The guiding light of the movement in Britain, the Fountain Trust, had been disbanded and the wise international statesman of the movement, David du Plessis, died of cancer in 1987. Moreover, serious splits had emerged as a result of the rapid growth of the house churches, later to call themselves the New Churches. The growth of the house churches had called into question the ecumenical vision of du Plessis with a new kind of 'come outism' which the early charismatics had previously rejected.

The New Churches shared a common experience with the charismatics and often shared the essentially middle-class origins of the charismatic movement as compared with the original working-class culture of the classical Pentecostals. Yet the vision of the house churches was rooted in a conviction that they heralded a revival that was to take place outside the historic churches and seemed to owe much more to older Pentecostal themes. Admittedly, the call of the house churches to 'restore' the New Testament church placed more emphasis on the significance of the church as a witnessing community than the older Pentecostal revivalism had done, but otherwise, many former Pentecostals found themselves very much at home in many of the new churches. Some of the key house church leaders had come from a Pentecostal rather than a charismatic past. Even more curiously, the charismatic leaders who welcomed Wimber to Britain seemed to have a greater degree of affinity with the New Churches than they had with the original vision of the charismatic movement. For all these reasons, the arrival of Wimber seemed to offer a means of reorientating a movement which in many ways seemed to have slightly lost its way.

What excited the leaders of the charismatic movement was not the idea that Wimber was speaking to evangelicals who didn't wish to become Pentecostals or charismatics, so much as their sense that the content of his message offered a powerful new direction to a movement which was badly divided and somewhat bereft of vision. Indeed, in Britain, Wimber's message was enthusiastically endorsed by those who already thought of themselves as charismatics.

The phrase most associated with Wimber and the Vineyard team in the early phase of their visits to Great Britain was that of 'signs and wonders', or as some observers sometimes gently rephrased it, 'signs and Wimbers'. In that early period, the single most important and controversial element was that of the healing ministry. The reason for this single focus on one aspect of Wimber's ministry lay in two closely-related realities. First, early introductions to Wimber's ministry tended to lay emphasis on the role of the miraculous as illustrated specifically by incidents of healing. John Gunstone's book *Signs and Wonders*, follows just such a pattern. Having described the beginnings of the Vineyard congregation, the account highlights the significance of one particular healing for Wimber's church and then continues:

'The congregation began to engage in the ministry of healing with greater faith, and its numbers increased.'[4]

Second, it became well-known in charismatic circles in Britain that one of its foremost leaders, David Watson, had gone to the Vineyard to be prayed for having developed cancer. Even though he was later to die from the same illness, the link between the healing ministry and Vineyard was firmly established in the minds of many associated with the charismatic movement in Britain.

However, Wimber was far from being a 'healing evangelist' in the traditional Pentecostal mould. The signs and wonders spoken of by Wimber were by no means confined to acts of healing even if such incidents were sometimes the most obvious and immediate manifestation of such wonders. Other such signs included the well-known manifestations of the Spirit which are commonly associated with the Pentecostal and charismatic movement, speaking in tongues, interpretation, prophecy, words of knowledge and occasionally the experience of falling over which is usually referred to as being slain in the Spirit. But if these encounters with the Spirit were no different from those which charismatics had known for years, why should Wimber not merely be seen as yet one more prominent leader of the same movement? Why the need to speak of something new?

Those who were themselves leaders in the charismatic movement sensed that something new was taking place but it was extremely difficult to delineate.[5] The difference had to be felt and experienced in order to be understood, but a partial definition is that it represented a qualitative difference in the expectation that God was going to move by the Holy Spirit.

John Gunstone records an insightful conversation between Wimber and an English bishop:

' "When I worship in English churches," John Wimber said to Richard Hare, the Bishop of Pontefract, at the Harrogate conference in 1986, "I detect in the congregations a remarkably high level of personal need, matched by a correspondingly low level of expectation." '[6]

The ministry of Wimber and his team seemed to be able to tap into this high level of need and produce equally high levels of expectation. I remember attending a Wimber meeting and becoming aware of the extent to which the simple invitation offered to the Holy Spirit to come and do what he desired to do, seemed to produce a sense of awe and wonder. It seemed to me then that it was a courageous thing to do. Yet within a very short time, slowly, quietly, there were unmistakable signs that God was at work in the congregation. It was a moving and inspiring occasion. There were no attempts to artificially create a sense of expectation. There were no loud and repetitive choruses, no altar call and no attempts to evoke an emotional response. If anything, the atmosphere that had been created was surprisingly low key, yet many who were in the congregation reported a feeling that God was present in power. The evidence that God was at work gave encouragement to those who had perhaps become somewhat worn out in the service of God.

The message, both spoken and assumed, was that this experience of God at work was not dependent on Wimber's presence but could be taken as normative for those who were prepared to reach out with similar levels of courage. In many ways, this kind of God encounter as the context of Wimber's ministry, was much more important than the context in which he was working. It seemed to me that in Britain the congregation was much more likely to consist of tired charismatics than evangelicals who did not wish to become charismatics.

The confident prayer of faith that underlies the invitation to God to come by his Holy Spirit is in fact a practical demonstration of that other ingredient which has come to be strongly associated with the ministry of Wimber and his Vineyard team – power evangelism. Wimber describes power evangelism as follows:

'By power evangelism I mean a presentation of the gospel that is rational but also transcends the rational. The explanation of the gospel comes with a demonstration of God's power through signs and wonders. Power evangelism is a spontaneous, Spirit-inspired, empowered presentation of the gospel. Power evangelism is that evangelism which is preceded and undergirded by supernatural demonstrations of God's presence.'[7]

For Wimber, the essential point of power evangelism is not that he and his team should conduct such demonstrations, though they do indeed attempt to model the signs and wonders that point to the power of God. It is much more that he expects every Christian to manifest such power in their everyday encounters with non-Christians. This emphasis shifts the focus from the large meeting to the personal relationships which Christians develop in their normal lives. The task of the Christian is therefore not merely to invite people to come and see signs and wonders performed but to engage with others in power encounters wherever they might find themselves. Signs and wonders are not just a means of adding spice to the worship experience but rather a basic empowering of lay people in such a way that Christianity becomes a genuinely lay movement.

Paradoxically, this ingredient in the teaching of Wimber relied heavily on insights gained from classical Pentecostalism as practised, not in the West, but in third world nations, particularly in South America. In this regard, Wimber once again owed a debt to Peter Wagner who was able to point him to the actual experience of the Pentecostals in Latin America, a dimension of Christianity which had previously escaped Wimber. Wagner had both visited and subsequently written extensively on Pentecostals in that continent. For Wimber, classical Pentecostalism in the Western world had become rather minister-dominated, with a significant reliance on the person and ministry of the pastor, or on occasion, the healing evangelist. His perception was that charismatics had become rather insular. Mission had tended to take second place to the renewal of the church without much subsequent impact on the wider world. In this sense, Wimber was legitimately reminding Pentecostals and charismatics in Britain of a neglected dimension in their own tradition. Pentecostals had once hoped for revival but what had come was only Pentecostal churches. Charismatics had once hoped for a renewal of the church which would lead to mission but what had come was often only a renewed style of charismatic worship.

By radically exploring that which should have been familiar to both Pentecostals and charismatics, Wimber was beginning to become aware of a kind of Babylonian captivity which had so far prevented either Pentecostals or charismatics in the West from breaking out of what had become simply a sub-culture within the Christian church. For Wimber, the heart of that captivity lay in the need for a profound shift in worldview, an insight for which he was indebted to the missionary and missiologist Charles Kraft.

The term coined by Wimber, but borrowed from elsewhere in missiological thinking, was the phrase 'paradigm shift'. Wimber's teaching relationship with the School of World Mission at Fuller meant that he was aware of the thinking of missiologists such as Paul Hiebert and Charles Kraft. Both of these thinkers had reflected on the significance of culture in the communication of the Christian faith. Their knowledge of other cultures was such that they could see a clear difference in the world view of those who lived outside the Western world as compared with those who lived within a Western worldview.

A worldview is sometimes described as what you think about the world when you are not really thinking.[8] In other words we imagine that the way we think about the world is the way things really are. When we meet those who see things differently then we can see the filters that they are using very easily, but seeing our own filters is much more difficult. It reminds me of the lady who spoke to me in a church in the American mid-west. In an accent so strong that it was almost a caricature of an American accent, she said to me, 'Gee, you got an accent!'

Wimber, together with his friends, Wagner, Kraft and Hiebert, saw only too clearly that a Western materialist worldview, heavily secular in its assumptions, simply could not hear the gospel in any meaningful sense. For mission to be effective, what was needed was not just better communication techniques but a means to help people change their minds at a much deeper level. The gospel simply could not be communicated while operating entirely on the basis of secular assumptions. A paradigm shift, in which basic assumptions about worldview could be challenged and changed, was therefore essential. The shift of assumptions is not necessarily the same thing as conversion but rather, an opening of one's mind to possibilities otherwise rejected so that a fair hearing can be given to the message of the gospel.

For Wimber, the power encounter with its signs and wonders represented a means of introducing such a paradigm shift. This is more than merely a matter of producing a healing or two. As many will be aware, while healings can produce astonishing responses in nations with a worldview closer to that of the Bible, in Western lands the same healings might only produce an acknowledgment that this represents an interesting subject for further investigation. The assumption is that any healing has operated entirely within natural, essentially material, categories, and that all that is required is a little longer to find out how it worked. A transcendent, spiritual dimension is ruled out even before investigation has begun.

The power encounter therefore is focused on bringing people to an actual God encounter in such a way that they are forced to rethink their basic categories for understanding the world. Witnessing unusual healings may be the start of such a process but actually it is a personal awareness of the dynamic presence of God that represents the centre of a paradigm shift. For those who have had a power encounter, nothing looks quite the same again.

The so-called third wave, with its talk of signs and wonders, power encounters, and paradigm shifts does represent a clearly different phase from that of classical Pentecostalism and the charismatic movement because the emphasis of the movement is clearly on mission in a first-world context. By contrast, Pentecostals in the Western world had talked largely of revival. For them, the Pentecostal movement was a revival outside a church which had rejected their message. But all talk of revival assumes a context of Christian understanding which in turn flows from a memory of Christendom. The very word 'revival' assumes that something dormant exists which can be revived. In revival the talk is of 'coming back to God' as if people had already been so that they might return. That set of assumptions was entirely justified in both the America and Britain of the early 20th century, but it is no longer the case.

The charismatic movement also assumes the presence of some form of Christendom. Its major focus is the church and not the unchurched. The Roman Catholic expert on the charismatic movement, Kilian McDonnell, has written of a debate which asks whether the participants in the renewal were formerly fully-committed Christians or only nominal ones.[9] There is no expectation in his writing that the participants will be completely new Christians. While Michael Harper and others hoped that the church would be renewed so that the world might later be evangelised, there is little evidence that there has been any such major outflow from the charismatic renewal.

Indeed, it was precisely the frustration at the lack of missionary zeal as an outcome of the charismatic movement, that prompted the invitation from English charismatic leaders to Wimber and the Vineyard team. These leaders were not looking for yet more renewal for church leaders and other committed Christians, they were looking for keys to taking the gospel beyond the boundaries of the church.

Wimber's background in church growth teaching allowed for a potent mixture of Pentecostal or charismatic experience with a strong practical evangelistic praxis. In part, Wimber's interest in Pentecostal phenomena was a recognition that it was a dimension that had powered unprecedented levels of church growth in overseas mission fields. Might it not be that such things could happen in the West? The Vineyard approach reveals a clearly applied philosophy taken from church growth teaching. The constructs of cell, congregation and celebration, so familiar to church growth advocates, are clearly present in the Vineyard structures. Other church growth categories also feature strongly in the life of Vineyard congregations.

It is easy to be a little cynical concerning what some have seen as the 'Vineyard franchise'. The application of certain methods, structures and philosophy to a church planting situation can seem rather artificial to British eyes, especially when applied to such details as coffee and doughnuts after the service. But behind this mixture of church growth thinking and Pentecostal practice lies a determinedly missionary priority. The congregations that are produced by the Vineyard philosophy are missionary centres, often, though not entirely, located in suburban centres so that they can reach out to larger centres of population beyond the immediate communities in which these congregations are set. Kingdom rearrangement is not the intention of the Vineyard leaders to whom I have spoken. Kingdom extension is. It is easy to make such pious statements but there is a reasonable degree of evidence to suggest that the actual practice of Vineyard congregations is orientated toward front-line evangelism.

Behind such an intention lies a clear missionary strategy which flows from Wimber's own thinking. Although one might expect a leader, who has been thoroughly imbued with the missiology of probably the world's leading centre for mission studies, to have a strong missionary orientation, the degree of sophistication revealed by Wimber is surprising. As early as 1987, Wimber's writing shows a thorough acquaintance with the work of Lesslie Newbigin in his analysis of the problems which an enlightenment worldview have brought to the task of mission in the West. American evangelicals are not noted for their acquaintance with the works of British ecumenical scholars and by 1987 few British church leaders of any persuasion were aware of the significance of Newbigin's writings. So, Wimber's understanding of the need for a paradigm shift is set firmly in the context of an analysis of Western culture which suggests that modernity is not just a problem for the gospel, it is itself another gospel, and one which had invaded the church itself.

Curiously, just as Wimber was accepting the analysis provided by Newbigin, almost undetected at that time, Western culture began another convulsion which has now attracted the problematic description of 'postmodernity'. Indeed, the secular landscape painted so accurately by Newbigin only really began to be called modernity as the term 'postmodernity' began to gain widespread currency. But it is precisely to the contours of postmodernity that Wimber's missionary praxis addresses itself. Almost above all else, postmodernity values the kind of experiential encounter with the universe which Wimber describes as power evangelism. The postmodern agenda has brought religion back onto the agenda of the Western world. But it is not the religion of the rational mind, the printed page and expository preaching. Rather it is the quest for a spirituality which encompasses the whole person. The healing of body, mind and spirit is easily understood by those standing in a postmodern mindset.

The context in which Wimber developed his approach to mission is undoubtedly significant. It is in the pluralistic culture of California as compared with the corporate culture of Chicago that Wimber has ministered. In many senses, Christianity helped to form the mid-west of America but it has almost always tended to stand at the margins of Californian culture. Wimber and the Vineyard have grown up in a mission field and that context has helped to shape their intuitive response.

It is unlikely in the extreme that the creation of more and more Vineyard fellowships will result in the re-evangelisation of Britain. But what is more certain is that the Vineyard congregations that are developing are offering genuinely missionary laboratories from which others may learn. Britain, Europe and the West in general need to see the emergence of many more missionary leaders and churches. Wimber's work and witness represents a helpful and significant inspiration in such a direction.

Notes

[1] There are many examples of this phrase in John Gunstone's book on Wimber but see particularly, Gunstone, John, *Signs and Wonders: The Wimber Phenomenon* (Daybreak, 1989, p 119).

[2] The Pentecostal statesman David du Plessis, was the first person to recognise that Pentecostalism was a spirituality and not necessarily a doctrine or a denomination. From that position he began to talk of Pentecost outside of Pentecost, as early as the mid-1950s. By this he meant that it was possible to have a pentecostal experience and yet remain outside Pentecostal denominations.

[3] Wimber, John, *Riding the Third Wave* (Marshall Pickering, 1987, p 31).

[4] Gunstone, John, *Signs and Wonders: The Wimber Phenomenon* (Daybreak, 1989, p 11.)

[5] When I was a young student, my Professor, Walter Hollenweger, recounted an experience which had taken place when he had first researched the Pentecostal movement.

He told me that he had visited a meeting which had been taken by a Pentecostal healing evangelist. When the time had come for the evangelist to preach, he had merely stood in the pulpit and begun to weep. As he did so, the Spirit swept across the congregation. Some also wept tears of repentance, others were slain in the Spirit, still others spoke in tongues and a number experienced healing. Having heard all this the Professor who was supervising Hollenweger's research said, 'Yes, but what did the preacher say?' Hollenweger replied, 'He didn't say anything.' The Professor was dumbfounded. From his point of view if nothing was said, then nothing had happened. He was a good reformed protestant!

[6] Gunstone, John, *Signs and Wonders: The Wimber Phenomenon* (Daybreak, 1989, p 70).

[7] Wimber, John, *Power Evangelism* (Hodder and Stoughton, 1985, p 46).

[8] Lesslie Newbigin describes it in such a way in a number of his writings.

[9] McDonnell, Kilian, *Presence, Power and Praise: Documents on the Charismatic Renewal* (The Liturgical Press, 1980).